The Executive's Guide To Corporate Responsibility Management and MVO 8000

Eugene A. Razzetti

authorHOUSE®

AuthorHouse™ LLC
1663 Liberty Drive
Bloomington, IN 47403
www.authorhouse.com
Phone: 1-800-839-8640

Published by AuthorHouse   07/18/2013

ISBN: 978-1-4389-2554-7 (sc)
ISBN: 978-1-4670-4626-8 (e)

Preface

The only thing necessary for evil to triumph is for good men to do nothing.
Edmund Burke

I think that I have wanted to write this book for over forty years. In that long expanse of time I have gone from pumping gas to U.S. Navy Captain, to military analyst and independent auditor and management consultant.

It is also in that long expanse of time that I have seen ethical management practices deteriorate across America, and with them the quality of American products, services, and reputations The Defense Industry, once the envy of the world, now decays, as contractors with friends in Congress produce poorer and poorer systems—later and later, and as costs go higher and higher. Americans follow their European counterparts into quality management systems, which, although excellent tools for the production line and factory floor, will not solve problems at the Boardroom level without the support and example of the Board. Environmental management systems are also excellent. However, they don't improve the <u>operating</u> environment—only the physical one.

Even among top management, where the highest standards should be set, the desire for monetary reward, and the measuring of greatness in terms of salary, power, and influence, sets companies on the road to mediocrity and disappointment. We watch as young executives willingly follow their bosses down a glittering road to irresponsibility, golden parachutes, and chaos.

This book contains no magic formulas, nor does it suggest that all other management books be thrown away. It will, however, help any organization to succeed in its mission by <u>identifying the right things to do,</u> gaining support and consensus inside and outside, and then accomplishing those same right things. Equally important to its success, the organization will set controls, know when it's going wrong, admit it, and go on to preventive and corrective measures.

The appendices at the end of the book contain the structure for an effective and ongoing Corporate Responsibility Management Program.

I include two excellent reference books on terrorism and emergency management. These topics are not specifically covered in the text, but they will be real management issues for the rest of our lives (mine at least), and these books should be required reading for the leader of any organization.

Having been blessed with strength and health, I have been working for over fifty years. I have always believed that the most effective management consultants come from Management, not from Consulting, and that the most effective managers go into academia, they don't come from it.

This is the second edition; revised to make your work easier. I welcome you to this book; and commend you on your decision to take on your corporate responsibilities. I am introducing MVO 8000 to you to give your programs measurable structure and accomplishment.

Lastly, I wish you every success.

Gene Razzetti,
Alexandria, VA

<u>*CEO Note.*</u> *Throughout the book will be flags for the CEO (like this), inviting his/ her attention to a special thought.*

TABLE OF CONTENTS

DEDICATION

I dedicate this book to my wonderful family and friends—living and deceased, to the United States Navy, where I learned the meaning of ethics and accountability, Mr. Bruce Weber, the CEO of QMS Global, Inc. and co-creator of MVO 8000, and to Professor Robert L. Canaan, who first introduced me to Management.

I also dedicate this book to you: the no-nonsense leader who sees the need to reintroduce and sustain measurable moral principles in your industry and in the USA.

Here's a quick look at what is available to you inside this book.

Topic or Document	Ready to Go In This Book
The MVO 8000 Standard	✓
Implementation Guidance and Explanation	✓
Code of Ethics & Standards of Conduct	✓
Template Corporate Responsibility Management Manual	✓
An Internal Audit Checklist	✓
Risk Management Spreadsheet Model Guidance	✓
Integration with other/exiting Standards	✓
Performance Metrics	✓

Now, let's get to work.

Gene Razzetti
Alexandria, VA

FOREWORD

__CEO Note.__ If you think a Corporate Responsibility Management System is expensive, try NOT having one.

More than ever, organizations need to recognize and accept all of the previously unseen responsibilities that involve good citizenship. It is neither easy, nor automatic. For an organization to be a good citizen, it must succeed across a spectrum of challenges that include (in addition to building a business):

- Community responsibility
- Employee health, safety and quality of life
- Environmental compliance.

In recent years, even the most overconfident CEOs have acknowledged the success of structured management systems like ISO 9000, ISO 14000, and many of the others. In those same recent years, monumental company failures have both underscored the need and created the requirement for CEOs and CFOs to satisfy themselves and attest in writing regarding the veracity of their documentation. Reliance on outsiders, to the exclusion of internal auditing and controls, inevitably leads to disaster.

This book introduces MVO 8000, which I had the privilege to help create. It is not the intention of this Standard to replace the knowledge and skill of the CEO with a cookbook. Rather, we intend to provide CEOs with useful tools to run their organizations as good leaders, managers, and neighbors.

MVO 8000 is applicable to any organization and can be efficiently integrated into existing management systems. It is derived from statutory and regulatory requirements, internal guidelines, best practices, and an *ethical imperative* to conduct business honestly and with proper regard for the employee, the customer, and the community. Its input requirements are essentially the same as for any other initiative to be effective, and as specified in international standards that continue to grow in popularity and contribution. Table 1 compares the requirements of MVO 8000 with proven International Standards.

Table1. Comparison of General Requirements of Popular Standards with MVO 8000

REQUIREMENT	ISO 9001	ISO 14001	ISO 27000	ISO 28000	MVO 8000
Standard and explanation	X	X	X	X	X
Top management involvement	X	X	X	X	X
Employee ownership	X	X	X	X	X
Reflected in Strategic Plan	X	X	X	X	X
Process Oriented	X	X	X	X	X
Resistance at first	X	X	X	X	X
Risk Assessment and Management	X	X	X	X	X
Training	X	X	X	X	X
Manual and checklists for structure	X	X	X	X	X
Capable of self-audit	X	X	X	X	X
Consolidates other standards and compliance requirements	X	X	X	X	X
Feedback loops	X	X	X	X	X
Corrective and Preventive action	X	X	X	X	X

MVO 8000 specifies the framework of a Corporate Responsibility Management System. It enables organizations to formulate policies and objectives governing company Corporate Responsibility, incorporating statutory and regulatory requirements, and the requirements of company personnel, stakeholders, suppliers, and the community. The Standard itself does not establish any specific ethical standards or values.

This Standard is applicable to every organization planning to:
- Implement, maintain, and improve a Corporate Responsibility System
- Comply with the established Corporate Responsibility policies
- Have its Corporate Responsibility System certified by an external organization and recognized worldwide
- Confirm by periodic audits that the Corporate Responsibility System is implemented and maintained in accordance with the Standard.

SECTION ONE— ELEMENTS OF CORPORATE RESPONSIBILITY MANAGEMENT

This section describes what it takes for an effective Corporate Responsibility Management System to the extent that a busy but experienced CEO (like you) can understand. It covers sections of MVO 8000 that are neither fully covered in the Standard or are not otherwise self-explanatory. More importantly, it was written to put the reader/executive in what we'll call a corporate responsibility management *mindset.* He/she will recognize in it the importance of the elements and their applicability across the broad spectrum of organization types and missions.

CORPORATE ETHICS

MVO 8000 defines *ethics* as the science concerned with systematic reflection on rules and issues—the way in which people act and the rules that form the basis of these actions.

Corporate Ethics, therefore, institutionalizes reflection on these rules and issues in the conduct of the business of the corporation. Corporate Ethics (or Corporate Responsibility Management) is the creation and control of the processes which ensure that corporations perform to established standards of ethical practice.

MVO 8000 can help your organization to discover, formulate, institutionalize and manage its corporate responsibility.

ORGANIZATIONAL CHARACTER— BECOMING THE BEST POSSIBLE NEIGHBOR

Unlike the more familiar standards, MVO 8000 works with the organization's *character* rather than of its *product*; in order to establish and continually enhance the total organization and the way that it does business. Specifically, MVO 8000 enhances the organization's ability to:

- ✓ Create a corporate culture that promotes ethical conduct and makes it a way of life
- ✓ Make a promise and keep it

- ✓ Pledge to a compliance requirement and meet it
- ✓ Be open and honest in all its dealings, with no trade-offs or cut corners
- ✓ Show the greatest possible respect to employees and customers
- ✓ Take seriously its responsibility to the community—however large or small
- ✓ Practice environmental husbandry and conservation
- ✓ Practice responsible risk management and critically and narrowly define acceptable risk
- ✓ Develop meaningful metrics and performance indicators
- ✓ Bullet-proof customer relationships
- ✓ Effectively self-audit, and not rely on outsiders
- ✓ Apply this organizational character to the future in both strategic planning and the selection and development of its next generation of leadership.

THE CORPORATE RESPONSIBILITY MANAGEMENT STANDARD—OVERVIEW

This Corporate Responsibility Management Standard covers relevant ethical aspects of business practice. Customers, suppliers, personnel, investors, and other "stakeholders" want to deal with a trustworthy organization that conducts its business with integrity. A reputation for trust and integrity is an irreplaceable management tool for recruiting and retaining high quality personnel. A structured corporate responsibility system will provide organizations with an agreeable, reliable, and ethically responsible working environment, providing the foundation for profitability and longevity. Not only will organizations be improved internally, but communities will be strengthened and enhanced.

MVO 8000 specifies the requirements for effective, self-sustaining, corporate responsibility systems. It was developed to be applicable to any organization, regardless of location, size, or purpose.

Implementation requires each organization to formulate policies, from which relevant procedures and standards are developed. Policy statements then transition into measurable goals and objectives. Feedback mechanisms (such as internal audits and management reviews) keep the system dynamic and flexible.

Risk assessments identify and prioritize where actions are required (or may have been ineffective). Relevant metrics monitor and measure interdependencies, and evaluate the effectiveness of preventive and corrective measures.

This Standard is not intended for the enhancement of, or change to, the statutory and regulatory requirements to which organizations must comply, nor is it meant to replace occupational safety and health, or environmental compliance regulations. However, a corporate responsibility management system, set up within an organization, can reinforce and give great credibility and cohesion to those areas.

Table 2 Comparison of Specific Clauses of ISO Standards with MVO 8000

ISO 9000	ISO 14000	ISO 27000	ISO 28000	MVO 8000
1.1 General 1.2 Process Approach 1.3 Relationship with ISO 9004 Compatibility with other management systems	Introduction	0.1 General 0.2 Process Approach 0.3 Relationship to ISO 9004 0.4 Compatibility with other management systems	4.4 Implementation and Operation	1.1 General 1.2 Policy and Procedural Requirements 4.7 Community Responsibility 4.8 Quality of Life 4.9 Competition
1. Scope 1.1 General 1.2 Application	1. Scope	1. Scope 1.1 General 1.2 Application	1. Scope	4 Managing the Corporate Responsibility Management System 4.2 Integrity and Disclosure
2. Normative References	2. Normative References	2. Normative References	2. Normative References	Introduction
3. Terms and Definitions	3. Terms and Definitions	3. Terms and Definitions	3. Terms and Definitions	Definitions
4.2 Documentation Requirements 4.2.1 General 4.2.2 Quality Manual 4.2.3 Control of Documents 4.2.4 Control of Records	4.4.5 Documentation Control 4.5.4 Control of Records	4.3 Documentation Requirements 4.3.1 General 4.3.2 Control of Documents 4.3.3 Control of Records	4.1 General Requirements 4.2 Security Mgmt Policy 4.3 Security Risk Assessment Planning 4.4.5 Document and Data Control	

ISO 9000	ISO 14000	ISO 27000	ISO 28000	MVO 8000
5. Management Responsibility 5.1 Management Commitment 5.2 Customer Focus 5.3 Quality Policy 5.4 Planning 5.5 Responsibility, authority, and communication	4.2 Environmental Policy 4.3 Planning	5. Management Responsibility 5.1 Management Commitment	4.3 Security Risk Assessment Planning 4.6 Operational Control 4.4.7 Emergency Preparedness, Response and Security Recovery	2 Management Involvement 2.1 Involvement of Management 2.2 Ethics Management Policy 2.2.1 Statutory and Regulatory Requirements 2.3 Administration and Management 2.3.1 Oversight Officer 2.3.2 Internal Communication 2.4 Management Oversight 3.3 Code of Ethics and Standards of Conduct
6 Resource Management 6.1 Provision of Resources 6.2 Human Resources 6.2.2 Competence, Awareness, and Training 6.3 Infrastructure 6.4 Work Environment	4.4.2 Competence, Awareness, and Training	5.2 Resource Management 5.2.1 Provision of Resources 5.2.2 Training, Awareness, and Competence	4.2.2 Competence, Training, and Awareness	3. Human Resources 3.1.1 General 3.1.2 Ethics Awareness Training 3.1.3 Complaints Procedure 3.1.4 Personnel Representation 3.2 Sanctions 4.3 Personnel Recruitment and Selection 4.4 Contracts of Employment 4.5 Performance Review 4.15 Competence, Experience, and Training
8.2.2 Internal Audit	4.5.5 Internal Audit	6 Internal ISMS Audits	4.4.5 Internal Audits	5.1.2 Internal Reviews
5.6 Management Review 5.6.1 General 5.6.2 Review input 5.6.3 Review output	4.6 Management Review	7 Management review of the ISMS 7.1 General 7.2 Review input 7.3 Review output	4.6 Management Review and Continual Improvement	

ISO 9000	ISO 14000	ISO 27000	ISO 28000	MVO 8000
8.5 Improvement 8.5.1 Continual Improvement		8 ISMS Improvement 8.1 Continual Improvement	4.6 Management Review and Continual Improvement	5 Metrics Establishment 5.1 General 5.1.1 Personnel, Customer, and Stakeholder Satisfaction 5.3 Continual Improvement
8.5.3 Corrective actions	4.5.3 non-conformity, corrective action, and preventive action	8.2 Corrective action	4.5 Checking and Corrective Action	5.2 Nonconformance and Corrective and Preventive Action
8.5.3 Preventive actions		8.3 Preventive action		

COMPATIBILITY WITH THE SARBANES-OXLEY ACT

CEO note: Your organization may not have to comply with SOX, but it wouldn't hurt to adopt the spirit, even if you don't have to adopt the letter. Whatever you decide, make sure that you can meaningfully measure and self-audit.

The Sarbanes Oxley Act (SOX) was passed in 2002 as a method for ensuring that publicly held corporations were more thorough and forthcoming in their governance and their documentation. This was the result of the abrupt and dramatic bankruptcy of several major corporations thought to be the very essence of excellence. CEOs and CFOs are now required to certify annual and quarterly financial reports as both *accurate* and *not misleading*.

Legislation such SOX and related Securities and Exchange Commission rules require companies to maintain internal controls, evaluate conditions, and to make accurate and forthright disclosures[1]. More than that, SOX forced top management to be more involved in its self-auditing, and not rely too heavily (to the point of exclusivity) on outside auditors.

Like SOX, MVO 8000 helps to identify and eliminate procedural gaps and voids that threaten sound company operation. Strong, cost-effective, internal

---

[1] The CEO/CFO must, by placing his signature on the document, attest to its correctness.

controls are optimal pursuits for companies and stakeholders, and essential to protect and preserve the livelihoods of all company personnel.

MVO 8000 addresses SOX requirements targeted at:

- Internal controls
- Enhanced management oversight and disclosure
- Collection and communication of information
- Risk identification and mitigation
- Gap analyses and corrective action.

CORPORATE RESPONSIBILITY MANAGEMENT POLICY

Corporate Responsibility Management policies cannot be "stand alone" statements. Instead, they must be integral to the mission, operations, and overall strategy of the organization. Policies already developed for pursuant to ISO 9000 or ISO 14000 (for example) are definitely appropriate for, and should be included in the policies developed in accordance with MVO 8000.

Management should develop Corporate Responsibility Management policies as a means of establishing its standards and leading the organization through their realization and continual improvement.

Corporate Responsibility Management policy development should:

- Clearly state management's commitment to high standards of ethical practice,
- Be consistent with management's vision and strategies for the future,
- Permit measurable objectives to be developed,
- Be widely disseminated within the organization and among other stakeholders,
- Document its objectives clearly and be reviewed routinely, and
- Be the object of continual improvement.

When determining Corporate Responsibility policy and objectives, management should consider the following:

- The expectations and needs of all interested parties,
- Involvement at all levels in the company,
- The importance of ethical awareness among all personnel,
- The resources necessary to achieve the objectives,

- The necessity of continuously improving the Corporate Responsibility management system,
- Communicating the Corporate Responsibility policy and objectives within, the organization,
- The determination of measurable objectives,
- The satisfying of statutory and regulatory requirements.

MORAL VALUES AND MORAL RESPONSIBILITY

CEO note: We act in this way because we know that it is <u>right and proper</u> to act in this way—for ourselves and our neighbors.

For simplicity, we can define moral values as the attaching of priority, importance, and allegiance to that which is morally good and correct. Having identified and stated our moral values, we need then to impose upon ourselves the responsibility to act in accordance with those moral values; specifically, the manner in which we conduct our business in the community and in the world.

RESPONSIBLE BUSINESS PRACTICE

Responsible business practice is more important now than in previous years. Until recently, environmental aspects (i.e., what an organization does that could potentially harm or endanger the environment) were the most prominent, and often the only thing that got management attention. The fundamental principles of responsible business practice are based on an integral and balanced development of what is called the "Triple P Concept": People (Corporate Responsibility), Profit (responsibly achieving profit) and Planet (environment) applied to all aspects of business.

Companies are challenged and measured by the ethical manner in which they do business. Company personnel, customers, consumer organizations, investors, environmental groups, employer and employee organizations constantly scrutinize the activities of companies.

Ethical reputations of companies have become as important as those earned for efficiency and profitability. Companies are learning the value of auditing themselves and not relying solely on external auditors. Companies must be able to explain to their customers, personnel, and society, the standards and values that they use when carrying out their business.

The objective of responsible business practice is, therefore, that companies balance productivity and efficiency with corporate responsibility, environmental attention, and corporate/community responsibility. Companies should suspend business with unprincipled or corrupt suppliers and sub-contractors, maintain a safe and intimidation-free working environment, and practice environmental management.

Company objectives determine the way in which profits are achieved. Company culture influences people's well-being and quality of life. Responsible Business Practice conforms to standards and values based on a company's operating interests, the interests of employees and the co-existence of those individuals in the company's work environment.

IDENTIFYING VULNERABILITIES

Like any of the more conventional subsets of organizational management, corporate responsibility management should be subject to the ongoing identification and assessment of vulnerabilities from within and from outside. The figure below describes a notional management assessment, the creation of which helps to prioritize management action and continuing improvement.

In figure 2, we assume that vulnerabilities will always exist and that aggressive CRM programs will decrease their magnitude and "harden" the organization. Accordingly, the goal of vulnerability assessment is to identify areas of low process protection and increase it where needed.

Figure 1 Vulnerability Identification

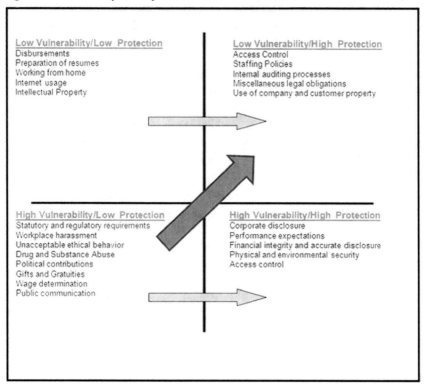

DETERMINING THE WORK TO BE DONE

I keep six honest serving-men. (They taught me all I knew); their names are What and Why and When and How and Where and Who. Rudyard Kipling

Having developed and stated our moral values and responsibilities, we then apply them to the organization. Ideally, the organization will reflect a history of morally correct performance, and likely will not require more than minor adjustment. In actuality, most organizations require more compelling action, These are organizations which either have no stated moral values or allow those values to exist as superficial and cosmetic place-holders; meaningless— both inside and outside the organization. Inevitably, these conditions manifest themselves in the organization's morale, efficiency, and profitability.

Figure 2 describes a notional organization. The extent to which these key +/- indicators are succeeding drives the amount of corrective action required.

Figure 2 Vulnerability Assessment

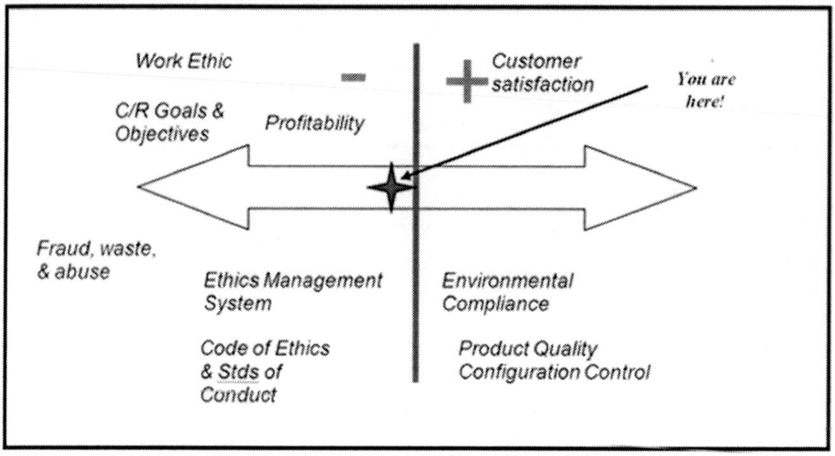

Customer satisfaction is positive because of an acceptable product. Environmental compliance is good because there is no allowable alternative. However, we see that profitability is driven downward, presumably as a function of problems with ethics management, fraud, waste, and abuse, and the Code of Ethics (or lack thereof).

There have been relatively few books written about the turnaround or resurrection of failing organizations, compared with texts assuming new or healthy organizations. Excellent books written on the subject of turnaround tend to focus on more quantifiable indicators (e.g., sales, purchasing, inventories,). We are assessing less quantifiable but equally important indicators, such as codes of ethics and standards of conduct, employee morale, and organizational goals and objectives. Since the goal is the same: to turn around an unsatisfactory situation, the approach is essentially the same as well: to identify vulnerabilities through a series of baseline assessments.

RISK MANAGEMENT

A successful Risk Management process requires:

- A flexible and general set of verbal, graphical, and mathematical tools supported (as necessary) by appropriate models or software.
- A family of related methods designed to suit the models, which link the models and the circumstances in which they are used.
- A wide range of relevant expertise and skills.
- The experience and leadership to design and integrate the models, organize the planning teams, and define and collect the desired objectives and findings of the analyses.

Risk assessment and minimization is currently recommended in the ISO 14001:2004 International Standard to evaluate and quantify (albeit subjectively) the environmental aspects of organizations and their potential impacts on the organization and the community.

Organizations will always be limited in the resources available to them and will need to identify their most likely problems, in order to prioritize those limited resources most effectively. Organizations should develop and use structured risk assessment, minimization, and management processes. This means assigning numerical values to probable outcomes of the different processes performed by the organization, the probability of consequence occurrence, and gravity of the consequences. Structuring like this creates risk "matrices".

Risk management can involve many different disciplines and areas of expertise—economics, finance, the environment, contracting, and a host of others—most having to do with major projects or industries. Not always considered is the potential benefit that risk management

(Or risk assessment, risk analysis, etc.,) has on design and planning processes for organizational ethics and corporate responsibility. It can also help with managing ethical risks and those affecting an organization's responsibility to the community. Organizations can and should develop these risk matrices themselves to evaluate potential ethical as well as environmental outcomes of different courses of action.

MVO 8000 can help your organization's risk management program by creating/enhancing:

- A flexible and general set of verbal, graphical, and mathematical tools supported (as necessary) by appropriate models or software.
- A family of related methods designed to suit the models, which link the models and the circumstances in which they are used.
- A wide range of relevant expertise and skills.
- The experience and leadership to design and integrate the models, organize the planning teams, and define and collect the desired objectives and findings of the analyses.

Table 3 contains the numerical values (1-10) and the corresponding criteria for computing risk assessment using Vulnerability, Criticality, and Threat.

Table 3 Risk Assessment Criteria

Level	Scale	Vulnerability Criteria	Criticality Criteria	Threat Criteria
Lowest	1, 2	Minimally vulnerable due to own resources	Minimally disruptive	Never occurred before; not a significant source of disruption
Low	3, 4	Susceptible, but physical surroundings make problem unlikely	Disruptive with minor degradation	Has occurred before; potential source of disruption
Medium	5, 6	Highly vulnerable due to limitations and physical surroundings	Mission degraded but can continue	Occurs periodically and predictably; disruptive when occurring
High	7, 8	Extremely vulnerable due to environment and physical surroundings	Mission seriously degraded; but can continue marginally	Occurs often; highly disruptive
Highest	9, 10	Imminent danger due to environmental and physical limitations	Mission failure; Much disruption	Limited utility and effectiveness against occurrence

Having established criteria and values for vulnerability, criticality, and threat, we describe a notional risk assessment matrix for environmental aspects in a shipyard in table 4. As shown in the table: ***Risk = Vulnerability x Criticality x Threat***

CEO Note: You can use a matrix like this to assess risk for any group of related processes in your organization.

Table 4 Notional Risk Assessment Matrix (Commercial Shipyard)

Process	Vulnerability	Criticality	Threat	Risk
Defueling	6	6	8	288
Dry docking	5	8	6	240
Sandblasting	4	8	4	128
Painting	4	6	5	120
Undocking	4	8	5	160
Refueling	6	5	7	210

In our example, it would appear that the greatest risk in the notional shipyard is in the defueling process prior to the ship entering drydock (288) and the least risk is in painting while in drydock (120)[2].

GAP ANALYSIS—WHAT'S HERE ALREADY AND HOW GOOD IS IT?

<u>*CEO Note:*</u> *You need to know your organization's situation. Benchmark, Benchmark, Benchmark!*

Industrial engineers often conduct variance analyses, or tests for significant differences between several mean values. This is (happily) not what we are talking about. For our purposes, gap analysis is the product of auditing the organization or specific processes with the checklists and approaches shown in the appendices. The analysis provides general indicators and not hard

---

[2] For a complete explanation of turning Risk *Assessment* into Risk *Management*, please see my other book: *Fixes That Last —The Executive's Guide to Fix It or Lose It Management.*

figures. You will be measuring gaps between what is expected and the actual conditions.

The next step after identifying the vulnerabilities is to measure their magnitude against an accepted standard or reference, then determine the "gap" between the desired and the existing. This is gap analysis.

The figure below describes the existence of a *gap* between expected and actual findings. Having identified the gap (using the associated metrics), we can then proceed to the gap analysis. That is:

> *Why* there is a gap or a difference between what could be reasonably expected and what actually occurs?
> *Where,* specifically, is the gap (i.e., what area or process)?
> *What* can be done to close the gap?
> o Is it reasonable, cost effective?
> > o Appropriate?
> > o Legal and ethical?
> > *How* do we measure the effectiveness of the corrective action (using the appropriate metrics)?

Figure 3 Gap Identification and Analysis

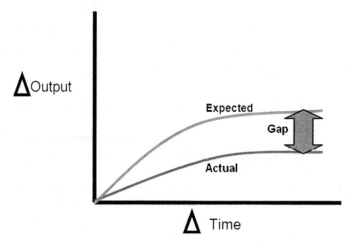

CONVERTING IDENTIFIED GAPS INTO GOALS AND OBJECTIVES—THE STRATEGIC PLAN

CEO Note: A critical consideration in the strategic planning process is the selection of (line and staff) participants; the greater degree of participation, the greater the degree of acceptance, accountability, and ease of facilitation.

There have been many excellent books written on the subject of Strategic Planning, and just as many that are trendy rather than excellent, and many consultants have been made rich ruining conference room walls with butcher paper and ink from magic markers. It is not the purpose of this book to repeat or contradict any of them. Neither is it our purpose to recommend your optimal approach to strategic planning (e.g., planning officers/staffs, teams, top down—bottom up). You decide the best approach; just ensure that you achieve the following results:

- You have a clearly defined mission for your organization
- You have a vision of how you will accomplish your mission
- You have identified your gaps.

Then, after identifying your gaps:

- You develop goals for your organization covering all pertinent areas of the mission and all areas in which gaps have been identified.
- You develop objectives, in which each of the identified goals is quantified in accordance with established metrics.[3]
- You develop a Plan of Action and Milestones (POA&M) from the objectives, assigning personnel/divisions by name, completion dates,
- You track the progress.[4]

It goes without saying (so why am I saying it?) that all of this requires buy-in from the employees. The Strategic Plan must belong to them as well as to you.

---

[3] A goal might be to reduce widget defects; an objective is to reduce widget defects by 10% each quarter.

[4] A POA&M for the above would be the Assembly Department Manager will cause a 10% defect reduction and report the status 30 June. Many organizations start with management-directed goals and never translate them into accepted and quantified objectives and milestones.

CREATING A VALUE BASE IN THE ORGANIZATION

CEO Note: Organizations must establish a value base for employees, suppliers, shareholders, and customers. Accordingly, it might be easier to think of creating a value base in the organization as a requirement, while long term profitability is a goal.

Creating a value base within the organization can consist of:

- Attracting and retaining good people, showing them (by word and deed) the importance of their contribution, and giving them the training and support needed to do their work well; and the attendant creation of a loyal, accountable, work force.
- Creating a corporate culture which encourages the optimum performance in all employees, regardless of how much effort went into retaining them.
- Seeking and retaining the most qualified suppliers, whose input is uniformly at or above a specified standard.
- Attracting customers who not only repeat their business, but refer your organization to new customers.
- Minimizing risk in the business processes, and the attendant reduction in the potential for lost customers, accidents, recalls, environmental damage, and the like.

DOING THINGS RIGHT

CEO Note: Ethical practices and economic effectiveness are not mutually exclusive. In the 1990s, many companies found that environmental management (not environmental compliance) lead to better looking bottom lines as well as better looking neighborhoods.

An organization intent on "doing things right" must make that intention actionable across a broad spectrum of its activities. Making a profit (as a likely example) means making it ethically. For example:

- Specifications were correctly developed and followed
- Prices were correctly determined
- Cost figures are accurate and proper
- Milestone inspections were performed and satisfactory
- Personnel training and competence are appropriate for the tasks and the environment (if not enhanced) was not damaged.

To achieve and maintain a reputation for doing things right, an organization must ensure that all of the above considerations (and more) are reflected in its delivery of products and services.

Add to this the need to be a good neighbor. Today's organizations must be ready to mobilize forces into structured acts of citizenship and commitment (e.g., adopt a school, park, or street).

INHERENT ETHICAL ISSUES

CEO Note: Day-in/day-out allegiance to your Corporate Responsibility Management System starts at the top—by example and not by fiat. Nothing spells disaster better than when your employees see you breaking rules that they would break at the cost of their jobs. You should already agree with this. If not, press the "I Believe" button and hold on a little longer.

Doing things right, as discussed earlier, involves an understanding of the ethical issues inherent in an organization. CEOs encounter these every day, when dealing with:

- Responsibilities to customers
- Responsibilities to suppliers
- Employee performance measurement and handling grievances
- Benchmarking ethical performance
- Product and service quality
- Community responsibilities
- Protecting the environment
- Employee recruitment, training, competence certification, health benefits, and general quality of life
- Ethical considerations in strategy development, marketing, and sales
- Internal auditing
- Development and certification of financial statements and disclosures.

RAISING THE LEVEL OF ETHICAL PERFORMANCE

THE CODE OF ETHICS AND STANDARDS OF CONDUCT

Organizations need to develop and publish what they consider to be ethical conduct by employees inside and outside the organization. Appendix Three is the Corporate Responsibility Checklist developed to help top management to identify and assess an organization's vulnerabilities. Here is a section from the checklist.

3.3 Code of Ethics and Standards of Conduct.

Has management created a Code of Ethics and Standards of Conduct, to include:

o *The Corporate Responsibility Management System,*
o *Statutory and regulatory requirements,*
o *Formal standards of performance and expectations,*
o *The organization's moral values with respect to personnel, customers, competitors, suppliers, and society,*
o *Unacceptable ethical behavior as it applies to the organization,*
o *Legal obligations of the organization and its members,*
o *Intellectual property,*
o *Physical and environmental security,*
o *Access control,*
o *Communications and operations management,*
o *Use of company property,*
o *Internet usage,*
o *Timesheet and travel claim preparation,*
o *Working from home,*
o *Internal auditing processes?*

*CEO Note. **We recommend that CEOs use the checklist in Appendix Three or one like it, in order to comprehensively assess vulnerabilities in the organization and to retain it as a record of the assessment.***

CORPORATE RESPONSIBILITY THUS FAR

This is a good time to stop and ask ourselves what Corporate Responsibility Management means up to now. At this point, we know the following:

- Black ink on the bottom line is not enough. There are other considerations and measurements
- You need to identify all the processes of the organization. Once identified, you need to understand the inherent risks to the product and the environment.
- You need to identify all your stakeholders. Certainly they include your employees, suppliers, shareholders, and community. They may be scattered all over the world, or just downstream of that little creek that flows behind your loading dock. You may be communicating with them with your very expensive website or with your storm drain.
- You need to identify all the ethical issues associated with your performance.
- You need to recognize your organization's ability to deliver value and the direct relationship its reputation has with that value.
- Day-in/day-out allegiance to your Corporate Responsibility Management System starts at the top—by example and not by fiat. Nothing spells disaster better than when your employees see you breaking rules that they would break at the cost of their jobs.
- Your responsibility to your employees and your suppliers goes beyond writing checks. You have an obligation to be fair and honest with them and a right to expect the same from them in return.
- You need to put your core values in writing.
- You put your name on your product, whether you realize it or not. You need to put your name on critical supporting documentation as well. Your products must be capable of measurement, and the measurement must be traceable.

Now, let's get back to work.

QUALITY OF LIFE

CEO Note: Improving your organization's quality of Life can be as complicated as a 401K or as simple as cleaning the restrooms more often. You need to involve yourself in the identification process. Think of Quality of Life as applying inside the organization and not to the neighboring community. Responsibilities to the community are discussed separately.

Management should recognize the organization's impact (positive or negative) on the quality of life of its personnel and identify and allocate resources as necessary. This can include:

- An initial benchmarking, as with a climate survey,
- Open meetings and communication, and
- Assessing the impact of other nonconformities in terms of personnel and community quality of life and including those assessments in management reviews.

LAWS, REGULATIONS, AND HUMAN RIGHTS

CEO Note: "To expect no regulation is willful blindness"—Peter Drucker

We have a history of manufacturing crises—unsafe automobiles, air and water pollution, hazardous waste disposal, and squandering of public utilities. This history has been chronicled in terms of deaths, diseases, public scandals, fines, product removals/recalls, and company bankruptcies; and also by government investigation, intervention, and legislation. When the government gets involved, it is usually after the damage is done and punitive action is the order of the day. It does not have to be that way, and forward-thinking organizations know that.

The public has the right to expect its products not only to be safe but to cause no harm in their creation; and the government has the obligation to ensure that right.

THE ENVIRONMENT IS EVERYBODY'S JOB

CEO Note: Mitigating or eliminating the product's impact on the environment does not have to mean raising the product's cost.

The International Environmental Management Standard known as ISO 14000 was adopted in the United States in 1996. It is not *a* standard but a *family* of standards, created in order for organizations to deal responsibly with their surroundings. *Control* means protecting the environment, improving it where possible, or allowing it to replenish or improve itself unabated.

Environmental Management is not Ecology nor is it Environmentalism. The reader can look up those definitions and see the dissimilarities. Neither is Environmental Management limited to environmental compliance, any more than safe, courteous driving is limited to remaining below the speed limit. Rather, it is proactive rather than restrictive and (in being so) allows imaginative managers to operate to their best advantages. Organizations need to define their environmental "aspects"—actual and potential, positive and negative.

An organization implementing a Corporate Responsibility Management System and not yet having an Environmental Management System can create both simultaneously. The organization should benchmark its initial situation relative to environmental compliance. It can effectively do this by conducting an assessment of its environmental compliance status with regard to:

- Hazardous material control and management
- Its activities and processes,
- Applicable statutory and regulatory requirements,
- Recycling and energy conservation,
- Supplier selection,
- Contract development,
- Development of environmental aspects.

THE SUPPLY CHAIN

The organization should establish documented processes to identify ethically responsible suppliers (including subcontractors) for purchased products or services and to routinely re-evaluate their continued performance; to include:

- Evaluation of competence,
- Performance against competitors,
- Contract adherence and quality of performance,
- Awareness of your organization's Corporate Responsibility Management system[5].

---

[5] Note: Clause 7.4.2: *Supplier Control Process* in the *ISO 9001:2008 International Standard* provides supplier quality standards. Adherence to those standards should ensure ethical performance of suppliers.

CORPORATE RESPONSIBILITY AND DELIVERING QUALITY SERVICE

CEO Note: "Nobody complains" is not enough (unless you manage a cemetery). Similarly it is also not enough that an organization commits only to not breaking any laws or knowingly making any unsafe products.

Delivering "quality" products and services on time and within budget has been the subject of many books, courses, standards, certifications, and (let's not forget) teambuilding workshops, thanks (most recently) to the work of quality giants like Juran, Deming, or Crosby.

Regrettably, implementations of quality management systems (however successfully) often confined themselves to the factory floor, and rarely impacted the executive suite. What is often lacking is the acceptance of quality management as a manifested sub-set of Corporate Responsibility Management.

Initially, (and appropriately) we consider the delivery of quality products and services as the sum of conformance to:

- Customer specification[6]
- Applicable safety laws and regulations
- Trade restrictions
- Environmental laws and regulations (i.e., doing no harm to the environment)
- Employee training and competence
- Internal and external feedback
- Correction of non-conformities
- Continuous improvement.

Additionally, there must be willingness on the part of the organization to attest (in writing) to the quality of the product or service, and then to place the reputation of the organization behind it. Specifically:

- The manner of its development
- The manner in which funds were expended and materials procured
- Open and honest product development and marketing
- Open disclosure of documentation (as required)
- An opportunity to protect or enhance the environment, as opposed to just doing no harm to it

---

[6] Including delivery schedules; a quality product delivered six months late and/or over budget is not a quality product.

- An open dialogue with the public (as required) [7].

It is in satisfying the latter that top management verifiably commits to its responsibility for its products or services, and it is at that moment when Ethics emerges as the definitive quality management system.

COST-BENEFIT ANALYSIS

Organizations now sensitized to Corporate Responsibility as well as to Strategic Planning can apply cost-benefit analyses to corporate responsibility situations, in order to determine the costs of new directions and (perhaps) reorganizations, compared with the projected benefits. Developing and applying cost-benefit equations allow managers to evaluate quantitatively potential initiatives or projects, and ensure that the benefits of corporate responsibility initiatives are greater than the costs.

There are many excellent books that teach cost-benefit analysis techniques. The best technique for you is the one that you customize for your organization.

METRICS ESTABLISHMENT

Just as with quality and environmental management systems, management should ensure that corporate responsibility management systems contain the means to measure and analyze ethical performance within the organization, identify deficiencies, and identify "actionable" improvements.

Examples of methods from which shortcomings can be identified and remedied include:

- Customer or employee satisfaction surveys
- Internal audits and reviews
- Organizational metrics (described herein)
- Self-assessment.

Management should ensure the establishment of an effective and efficient internal review process to assess the strengths and weaknesses of the System. Measurement processes provide independent tools for obtaining *objective evidence* about the operation of the organization.

---

[7] "Services" don't always undergo the same scrutiny as actual products. As a military analyst, I reviewed many tactical procedures, standard operating procedures (SOP), and assorted doctrine created by contractors for U.S. Forces in Iraq. Contractors pressured inexperienced/over-tasked Service members to take ownership, and some of these documents could only be described as criminally deficient.

Management should also consider establishing self-assessment mechanisms to supplement audit evidence regarding the Corporate Responsibility Management System.

INTERNAL REVIEWS AND AUDITS

CEO Note: Incorporate the checklists in the back of this book into your internal auditing strategy, whether or not you are already operating under an ISO standard. With any luck, you'll find that you are already doing much of what the checklists recommend.

The ability of an organization to detect, react to, and correct a shortcoming is one of the best ways to impress stakeholders. Whether you call them internal audits, reviews, controls, or (if you've done some time in the Military) inspections, these self-imposed forays into how you do your business are among the single most important actions that you can take to keep your organization safe, legal, profitable, and responsible. Internal reviews (let's use that term) let you find the shortcomings before they become obvious on the outside. They can be as complex or as basic as they need to be. It's only important that they fully address the subject or process and that the shortcomings uncovered are acted upon. Reviewers should not be reviewing their own work, but they should fully understand the subject matter that they are reviewing.

As discussed earlier and in the references, SOX was created because companies with fiduciary responsibilities to stakeholders were not self-auditing, or at least not doing it fully or providing written assurance that it was being done.

For purposes of MVO 8000 and Corporate Responsibility Management, we defined an *audit* as a systematic and independent survey to determine whether or not activities carried out in the area of company ethics, and the corresponding results achieved, conform to statutory and regulatory requirements, have been implemented effectively, and are appropriate to achieving the objectives.[8]

The internal review requirements of MVO 8000 are essentially the same as the internal auditing requirements of ISO 9000. Both standards believe that the most effective organizations are those that audit, and that the most effective audits are those that organizations do for themselves. If you already have one of the ISO standards in effect, then you can easily add MVO 8000

---

[8]   Again, terms like "audits"," reviews", or "controls" can be used interchangeably.

requirements to the same audit strategy. If you are just getting into self-auditing, the checklists in the back of this book will get you jump-started.

Outreach into the Community

CEO Note: "*The business that is too big, especially the business that is too big for the local community, is a threat to its community but, above all, to itself. It is incumbent on management to correct the situation in the interest of the business, To ignore the problem is to put ego, desire for power, and vanity ahead of the good of the institution and the community*"—*Peter Drucker*

Management must identify and assess its impact on the community. Its first two assessments are:

- Whether or not it is doing what it was established to do; and
- Whether or not it is doing what the public expects.

Assuming that those two assessments are successfully passed, organizations can do many things that not only enhance their standing in the community but their profitability as well. In addition to being consistent with the organization's mainstream practices, outreach into the community pays dividends in many ways, including:

- Achieving competitive advantage
- Making the organization more attractive to both customers, suppliers, and potential employees
- Building team spirit
- Improving management self-confidence and communication skills
- Problem solving
- Establishing/promulgating the organization's common core values and commitment
- Reducing organization-community resistance
- "Banking" goodwill
- Establishing track records (e.g., on-time deliveries)
- Building relationships and networks
- Raising educational levels (adopt-a-school, student placement, mentoring).[9]

An organization should fully define its roles, responsibilities, and authorities as a member of the community, to include:

- Identification of environmental aspects of operation,

---

[9] Sometimes called Corporate Community Involvement (CCI)

- Assignment of monitoring duties to a management representative,
- Periodically evaluating performance of community responsibilities as part of the Management Involvement process,
- Execution of policies and objectives,
- Development of recommendations for improvement and appropriate feedback mechanisms, and
- Normal and emergency lines of communication.

BEST MANAGEMENT PRACTICES

CEO Note: Sacred cows make the best hamburger!

Best management practices, over the years have generally come to mean what works best for the organization. They can refer to products, services, or the indirect operation of the organization. Best management practices, like processes developed under ISO 9000 for example, should be subject to review with thought to continuous improvement through periodic review and revision. Subjecting these practices to cost-benefit analysis (see above), or with thought to the environment (e.g., recycling) will likely cause their revision, even if only slightly.

The review of best management practices with thought to Corporate Responsibility Management is also likely to result in some revision of those practices to the betterment of the organization and the community.

Top management must encourage in the organization the conviction that every process, regardless how venerable or highly sited, can be improved and, by that improvement, better the organization and its stakeholders.

BUILDING TRUST IN RELATIONSHIPS

CEO Note: Top management has learned that its perception of reality does not always accurately reflect actual operations, processes, and interactions.

Your stakeholders trust you to know your business and to conduct it in a wholly responsible manner. That said, how good are you at doing your whole job, and do you and your senior managers justify that trust? See if you can comfortably answer the following questions:

- How much do you and your senior managers know about the day-to-day operations of your organization?
- How much more should you know?

- How credible a defense is ignorance of an occurrence, condition, or situation if there should have been an effective auditing, inspection, or reporting system followed?
- How qualified are you and your senior management in knowledge areas such as corporate law, occupational safety and health, pollution prevention, and generally accepted accounting practices?
- Do you believe that top management should lead by example, or are there separate sets of values?

STRATEGIC VERSUS OPERATIONAL CORPORATE RESPONSIBILITY

CEO Note: It's not just about making a profit anymore.

Here are some considerations as you prepare to embrace Corporate Responsibility for the long haul.

- Today's organizations have more stakeholders than ever before, because the definition has been expanded. You need to identify all of yours.
- There are many regulations dealing with occupational safety and health and the environment. You need to know those that affect your organization and operations. You may also need to know the status of your suppliers with regard to those same regulations.
- Your employees expect you to empower them as well as to direct them.
- Teams are growing and middle management is declining. Don't let Accountability fall through the cracks.
- Competition is global and the loyal, steadfast, customer just went on the Endangered Species List.
- Government involvement is increasing. That's bad.
- Consumers and the general public are more critical of their products than in previous years.
- Organizations certified in ISO 9000, ISO 14000, and others are growing in numbers and are (rightly) gaining competitive advantage.
- Networks are increasing in importance, and in doing so, increasing your vulnerability to natural and man-made attacks.
- Company loyalty is decreasing as the inverse of executive movement.
- Ethical, safety, and environmental responsibilities are as important and as unrelenting to CEOs as their financial responsibilities.

DOCUMENTATION FOR CORPORATE RESPONSIBILITY

CEO Note: Your documentation system need be little more (in quantity) than you are already doing. You should ensure that your documentation defines, implements, and maintains the Corporate Responsibility Management System, and supports effective implementation and execution of all of the organization's processes. Think "management tools" not "recurring reports".

Documentation that satisfies the needs of personnel, customers, society and stakeholders should include:

- The contractual requirements of personnel, customers and stakeholders;
- The acceptance of international and national standards;
- National and international laws and regulations (as applicable);
- Information and feedback on the needs and expectations of personnel, customers, stakeholders and the community; and
- Relevant external information sources.

Documentation should be developed based on:

- Functionality,
- User friendliness,
- Statutory and regulatory requirements,
- Control,
- Necessity.

TRAINING FOR CORPORATE RESPONSIBILITY

CEO Note: Top management needs to not only "train" subordinates, but to lead by example. A corporate responsibility "mindset" must permeate the organization, or else training will be meaningless. Worse yet, cosmetic!

Consider these questions:

1. When can senior management (and therefore the organization) be held accountable for offenses committed by junior personnel who have broken the company rules but have not been properly trained, selected instructed, or supervised?
2. Is ignorance a credible defense?
3. What level of competence is expected?

An effective ethics awareness training program, supplied by a Management that practices what it preaches, can reduce undesirable or inappropriate behavior by employees. For purposes of this Standard, we define ethics awareness training as *customized training dealing with unethical, unsafe, or undesirable practices in the organization, and how those practices impact on organizational performance and morale.* Management should ensure that its ethics awareness training program includes the following objectives:

- Building awareness of ethical standards and values of individuals and communities;
- Formulating/maintaining a Corporate Responsibility policy and (measurable) objectives;
- Developing and documenting of a code of ethics and standards of conduct; development and implementation of a Corporate Responsibility management system;
- Responsible Business Practices; and
- Communication and interactive skills.

CREATING SATISFACTION VS. AVOIDING DISSATISFACTION

CEO Note: It will not be enough to avoid dissatisfaction among your stakeholders. If you are intent on creating satisfaction, you will need to reach for the positives. If "zero" is your goal, the stakeholders will pull up stakes.

Creating satisfaction requires the involvement and support of everybody in the organization. This is best done by:

- Ongoing training and career planning,
- Defining all responsibilities and authorities,
- Establishing individual and team objectives,
- Recognition and reward,
- Encouraging open, two-way communication,
- Continually monitoring the needs of the employees and measuring satisfaction,
- Encouraging effective teamwork,
- Reviewing reasons for joining or leaving the organization.

It is in the creation of policies and practices that underpin your highest ethical visions and goals that you will make true corporate responsibility progress. Aiming only to avoid dissatisfaction is like setting your sights on Purgatory—you'll fall short[10].

---

[10] Sister Mary Discipline used to advise me like that—right before I got belted.

BENEFITS OF A CORPORATE RESPONSIBILITY MANAGEMENT SYSTEM

CEO Note: This is not entirely a shameless plug for MVO 8000, which I helped to create and am very proud of. You need something.

These are the reasons that I believe organizations need a structured corporate responsibility management system like MVO 8000. Here is part of a presentation that I have made to tout my product. The bullets need no further explanation.

A. General benefits of a Corporate Responsibility Management System

- Better risk and crisis identification and management
- Better relations with stakeholders and interested communities
- Increased worker commitment
- Increased productivity potential
- Reduced operating costs
- Enhanced brand value and reputation
- Long-term sustainability for company and society.

B. Specific benefits of MVO 8000

- Internal
    - A comprehensive Ethics Management System
    - A Code of Ethics and Standards of Conduct
    - Prevention of ethics, safety, or environmental violations
    - The ability to self-audit

- External
    - Certification to an established standard by an international registrar
    - Recognition and image enhancement
    - A unique and unequalled marketing tool—ahead of its time
    - Measurably improved customer and community relations.

PREPARING FOR A CORPORATE RESPONSIBILITY STANDARD—TIME TO GET TO WORK

Chart 1 provides an overview of the Corporate Responsibility Management System establishment and installation process. We have discussed the main points. Now, note the input and output arrows and the feedback. Like the ISO systems, Corporate Responsibility in general and MVO 8000 in particular stress continual improvement. It is understood that systems and processes should be subject to structured review and that every process can always be made better.

Chart 1 Establishing a Corporate Responsibility Management System

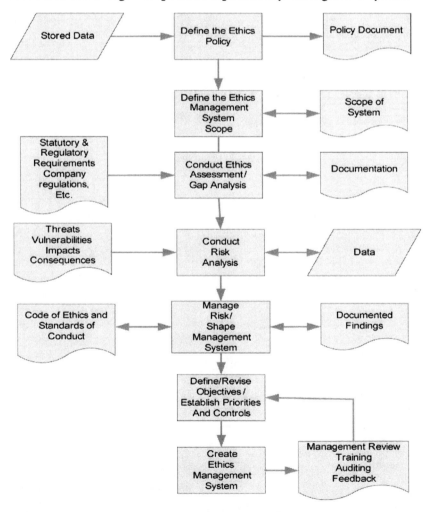

HIRING A CONSULTANT

CEO Note: Be careful what you delegate. The Consultant cannot take your place, or even give the appearance of taking your place. YOU must take a hands-on approach, involving yourself in every step of the implementation process.

As a management consultant, I believe that there is nothing I can do that the CEO could not do on his or her own. However, the CEO often cannot take the required time. More important, the CEO does not have the detachment that is needed to impartially assess the state of the organization to the satisfaction of the CEO, the Board, or the stakeholders.

Here is how I envisioned helping organizations to implement a Corporate Responsibility Management System like MVO 8000.

Chart 2 Using a Consultant to help establish your Corporate Responsibility Management System

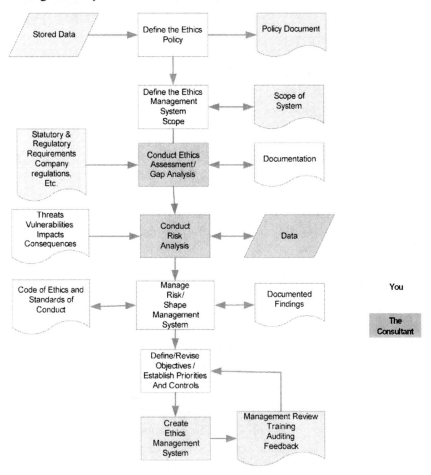

The Consultant that you engage should:

- Be a management consultant with demonstrated capability to put himself in your position. A specialist in one area (e.g., HRM or Sales) may not be able to help you tie it all together.
- Lay out the entire project and identify all requirements and resources. The project should (like Chart 2) describe what will be done, by whom, and when. Chart 2 is an example. Your organization may, depending on many factors, take a different approach. Chart 2 is not sacred, it's one approach.
- Determine at the outset what has already been developed, its effectiveness, and whether or not it requires modification or revision. This is gap analysis and the benchmarking.
- Advise you and your team, but make no decisions.
- Be willing to assist in the implementation process, let your people work out the kinks, then come back to make whatever modifications are required.

CONTINUAL IMPROVEMENT

The ISO Standards require a continual improvement strategy and mindset. The premise being that everything that the organization does is capable of improvement, and you should expect to periodically review and revise whatever you create, however robust it may appear at the time.

Management should create a culture of continual improvement, to sensitize employees to the importance of ever-higher standards of ethical conduct and encourages them to seek opportunities to improve ethical performance. Management can achieve and maintain a state of continual improvement by:

- Practicing what it preaches
- Setting objectives within the organization,
- Benchmarking own and competitor performance,
- Recognition and reward for achievement of improvements, and
- Including suppliers in the improvement processes.

SECTION TWO—SYSTEM REQUIREMENTS

The MVO 8000 International Standard follows. The actual standard is shown in italics and follows the guidance sections for each clause[11].

CORPORATE RESPONSIBILITY SYSTEM REQUIREMENTS

1.1 *General*

Management is expected to define, implement, and maintain the Corporate Responsibility Management System, and also to support effective implementation and execution of the organization's processes.

Documentation that satisfies the needs of personnel, customers, society and stakeholders should include:

- The contractual requirements of personnel, customers and stakeholders;
- The acceptance of international and national standards;
- National and international laws and regulations;
- Information on the needs and expectations of personnel, customers, stakeholders and the community; and
- Relevant external information sources.

Documentation should be developed based on:

- Functionality,
- User friendliness,
- Statutory and regulatory requirements,
- Control,
- Necessity.

Documentation can be produced in any form or medium suitable for meeting the needs of the organization.

The organization will set up and maintain a Corporate Responsibility Management Manual, which contains:

- The areas of application of the Corporate Responsibility Management System,

---

[11] Please check the draft Corporate Responsibility Management Manual contained in Appendix V.

- The procedures that have been determined and documented for the Corporate Responsibility management system.

1.1 General

The organization will develop, document, implement, and continually improve a Corporate Responsibility System relevant to its business operations. Specifically, the organization will:

a) *Monitor, measure, and analyze the System*
b) *Implement corrective and preventive action as necessary.*

1.2 Policy and Procedural Requirements

1.2.1 General

Corporate Responsibility System documentation will consist of an ethics manual containing documented explanations of ethics policies and objectives, and procedures required by this Standard.

1.2.2 Corporate Responsibility Management System Policy Manual

Organizations should establish a Corporate Responsibility Management System Manual that:

- Defines the scope of the Corporate Responsibility Management System in the organization
- Promulgates specific procedures for system operation and maintenance
- Summarizes relevant statutory and regulatory requirements
- Describes the interaction of the Corporate Responsibility Management System with other management systems and organizational activities, including dealing with suppliers.

1.2.2 Corporate Responsibility Management System Policy Manual

The organization will establish and maintain a Corporate Responsibility System policy manual that includes:

a) *The scope of the Corporate Responsibility System,*
b) *The documented procedures established for the system or reference to them, and*

c) *A description of the interaction between the processes of the*
Corporate Responsibility System.

---

2. MANAGEMENT INVOLVEMENT

The responsibilities of management with regard to the development and maintenance of a Corporate Responsibility Management System are essentially the same as those any management system. Organizations realize that success or failure of quality management systems can be quantified. Management's ethical responsibilities with regard to the environment are also quantifiable. The table provides examples.

Audit Area	Indicator	Measurement	Desired Trend
Quality	Scrap/re-work	Pieces/day	Down
Environmental	Hazardous Waste Energy Costs	Gallons/year Kilowatt Hours	Down Down
Morale	Absenteeism	Labor hours	Down
Contract fraud	Legal action	Incidents	Down
Employee sanctions	Inappropriate action	Incidents	Down

Management's operation of its stated corporate responsibilities requires that it establish performance metrics and routinely assess company activities in accordance with those metrics. Additionally, management must act on the findings of those metrics, assign responsibilities, implement corrective actions, and follow up on the effectiveness of those corrective actions.

2.1 Involvement of Management

Management will demonstrate its ethical involvement with respect to customers, suppliers, company personnel, external board members (as applicable), other stakeholders, and the community by:

a) *Communicating to all levels in the organization the importance of satisfying the requirements, standards, and values used by the organization to carry out its business,*

b) *Communicating to all levels in the organization the importance of satisfying statutory and regulatory requirements in the practice of company ethics,*

c) *Implementing the company's ethics policies and objectives,*

d) *Carrying out a program of internal reviews.*

2.2 Corporate Responsibility Management Policy

Corporate Responsibility Management policies cannot be "stand alone" statements. Instead, they must be integral to the mission, operations, and overall strategy of the organization. Policies already developed for pursuant to ISO 9000 or ISO 14000 (for example) are definitely appropriate for, and should be included in, the policies developed in accordance with MVO 8000.

Management should develop Corporate Responsibility Management policies as a means of establishing its standards and leading the organization through their realization and continual improvement.

A Corporate Responsibility Management policy development should:

- Clearly state management's commitment to high standards of ethical practice,
- Be consistent with management's vision and strategies for the future,
- Permit measurable objectives to be developed,
- Be widely disseminated within the organization and among other stakeholders,
- Document its objectives clearly and be reviewed routinely, and
- Be the object of continual improvement.

When determining the Corporate Responsibility policy and objectives, management should consider the following:

- The expectations and needs of all interested parties,
- Involvement at all levels in the company,
- The importance of ethical awareness among all personnel,
- The resources necessary to achieve the objectives,
- The necessity of continuously improving the Corporate Responsibility management system,
- Communicating the Corporate Responsibility policy and objectives within, the organization,
- The determination of measurable objectives,

- The satisfying of statutory and regulatory requirements.

2.2 Corporate Responsibility Management Policy

Management will determine a policy and ensure that the policy formulated:

a) *Is suitable and contiguous with the needs of the organization,*
b) *Is consistent with statutory and regulatory requirements,*
c) *Provides for continuous improvement of the Corporate Responsibility System.*

2.2.1 Statutory and Regulatory Requirements

The organization will identify statutory and regulatory requirements applicable to its operations.

2.3 ADMINISTRATION AND MANAGEMENT

Responsibilities and authorities

Management should make known within the organization, all tasks, responsibilities, and levels of authority needed to implement and maintain an efficient and effective Corporate Responsibility Management System.

All employees in the organization should understand their responsibilities to contribute to achieving the formulated objectives.

2.3 Administration and Management

Management will establish:

a) *The tasks, responsibilities, and authorities of all employees with respect to carrying out the formulated ethics policy*
b) *The tasks, responsibilities, and authorities of assigned supporting contractors, as applicable.*

2.3.1 Oversight Officer/Management Representative

An Oversight Officer should be appointed by the Chief Executive, who will then delegate to him/her, the authority to manage, monitor, assess, and coordinate the System. The Oversight Officer should communicate with, and report to, the Chief Executive and senior executives, and may, at the discretion of the Chief Executive, communicate with personnel, boards and stakeholders about matters concerning the System. The Oversight Officer need not be the Management Representative for other management systems formed pursuant to other standards (e.g., ISO 9000 or ISO 14000).

2.3.1 Oversight Officer/Management Representative

Management will appoint an individual responsible for the development, implementation, and maintenance of the Corporate Responsibility System; who reports directly to the Chief Executive and periodically reports on the performance of the Corporate Responsibility System and identifies potential improvements.

2.3.2 Internal Communication

To strengthen the involvement of the personnel, management should develop and maintain open communication regarding Corporate Responsibility policies and objectives as they apply in the organization. For example:

- Setting up training and indoctrination sessions for the personnel,
- Putting information on the website or network,
- Periodically placing information in the personnel magazine or newsletters;
- Providing information via e-mail and/or websites,
- Ensuring that the Corporate Responsibility policy is a fixed agenda point in the regular meetings.

2.3.2 Internal Communication

Management will provide a structure to inform personnel about the Corporate Responsibility System, in which communication takes place at all levels and functions regarding the effectiveness of the Corporate Responsibility System.

2.4 Management Oversight

Management oversight meeting frequency should be determined by the needs of the organization. The input from these meetings should provide output which will eventually lead to an improvement in the performance of the System.

— — — — — — — — — — — — — — — —

2.4 *Management Oversight*

Management will periodically review the effectiveness of the Corporate Responsibility Management System. Management will determine:

   a)   If the System has to be modified,

       b)   If policies have to be modified, or objectives amended,

       c)   The need for (or status of) corrective and preventive actions.

3.   HUMAN RESOURCES

3.1 Human Resources

Management should involve all personnel in the implementation and execution of the Corporate Responsibility Management System by increasing the level of Corporate Responsibility awareness. Management should determine the resources needed to achieve Corporate Responsibility objectives and ensure that they are made available.

— — — — — — — — — — — — — — — —

3.1.1 *General*

Personnel will be trained on the Corporate Responsibility Management System, its importance to the ethical operation of the organization, and how it applies to their positions and functions.

3.1.2 Ethics Awareness Training

An effective ethics awareness training program can reduce undesirable or inappropriate behavior. For purposes of this Standard, we define ethics awareness training as customized training dealing with unethical, unsafe, or undesirable practices in the organization, and how those practices impact on organizational performance and morale. Management should ensure that its awareness training program includes the following objectives:

- Building awareness of ethical standards and values of individuals and communities;
- Formulating/maintaining a Corporate Responsibility policy and (measurable) objectives;
- Developing and documenting of a code of ethics and standards of conduct; development and implementation of a Corporate Responsibility management system;
- Responsible Business Practices; and
- Communication and interactive skills.

3.1.2 Ethics Awareness Training

Management will:

a) *Develop and schedule Corporate Responsibility awareness training for all personnel,*
b) *Record and evaluate all training activities related to the Corporate Responsibility System.*

3.1.3 Complaints Procedure

Organizations require a documented complaints procedure for employees to report unsafe or unethical conditions in the workplace without fear of exposure or retribution.

3.1.3 Complaints Procedure

Management will provide employees with a process for communicating instances of unacceptable behavior, to include:

a) *The complaint submission procedure*
b) *Responsibilities for complaints procedure administration,*
c) *Confidentiality of complaints,*
d) *Appeal rights of personnel accused.*

3.1.4 Personnel Representation

Management should form a structured and documented personnel representation body, whose purpose is to:

- Contribute to the functioning of the organization,
- Look after the interests of all employees as they are influenced by the Corporate Responsibility Management System.

The personnel representation body should maintain records of meetings and actions taken or recommended as a result of those meetings.

— — — — — — — — — — — — — — —

3.1.4 Personnel Representation

Management will create a committee within the organization:

a) *To monitor the ethical functioning of the organization,*
b) *To define objectives, tasks, responsibilities, authorities, and procedures in the operation of the Corporate Responsibility System, and*
c) *To review instances of reported violations, and*
d) *To administer the organization's sanctions (see 3.2).*

3.2 Sanctions

To control and prevent undesirable behavior, organizations should implement documented systems within which undesirable behavior can be either prevented or corrected. This section describes the scope of the sanctions procedure.

— — — — — — — — — — — — — — —

3.2 Sanctions

In order to manage and prevent unacceptable ethical behavior, the organization will develop a system of sanctions to include:

a) *Definition and description undesirable ethical behavior in the organization,*
b) *The manner in which unacceptable ethical conduct is reported,*
c) *The manner in which corrective action will be taken, and*
d) *The manner in which personal information is documented and recorded.*

3.3 Code of Ethics and Standards of Conduct

Organizations cannot expect compliance with a Corporate Responsibility management system if the governing principles of that system are not fully stated and understood by all assigned personnel. Moreover, the procedure by which the principles are imparted on the personnel must be structured to include a structured procedure in which personnel receive training and signify in writing their understanding and willingness to comply. Toward that end, organizations should develop comprehensive, documented, codes of ethics and standards of conduct.

Personnel will be trained, initially and periodically, on the Code of Ethics and Standards of conduct and will sign an appropriate record affirming their understanding and compliance.

3.3 Code of Ethics and Standards of Conduct

Management will create a Code of Ethics and Standards of Conduct, to include (as applicable):

a) *The Corporate Responsibility System*
b) *Statutory and regulatory requirements*
c) *Financial integrity and accurate disclosure*
d) *Formal standards of performance and expectations*
e) *Harassment*
f) *Staffing policies*
g) *The organization's approach to personnel customers, competitors, suppliers, and community*
h) *Unacceptable ethical behavior as it applies to the organization*
i) *Legal obligations of the organization and its members*
j) *Intellectual property*
k) *Physical and environmental security*
l) *Access control*
m) *Proper recording or and disbursement of funds or other assets*
n) *Use of company and customer property*
o) *Internet usage*
p) *Drug and substance abuse policy*
q) *Public communication*
r) *Working from home,*

s) Internal auditing processes

t) Political contributions

u) Preparation of resumes

v) Wage determinations and gifts and gratuities.

---

4 MANAGING THE CORPORATE RESPONSIBILITY MANAGEMENT SYSTEM

4.1 Communication and Participation

Effective corporate responsibility management requires the involvement and support of all personnel in the organization. This is best done by:

- Ongoing training and career planning,
- Defining all responsibilities and authorities,
- Establishing individual and team objectives,
- Recognition and reward,
- Encouraging open, two-way communication,
- Continually monitoring the needs of the employees and measuring satisfaction,
- Encouraging effective teamwork,
- Reviewing reasons for joining or leaving the organization.

4.1 Communication and Participation

Management will involve all levels of the organization in the operation of the Corporate Responsibility System.

a) *Committees will ensure that meetings are recorded, and*

b) *Sufficient time and resources are allocated.*

4.2 Integrity and Disclosure

MVO 8000 addresses Sarbanes-Oxley Act requirements dealing with:

a) Internal controls

b) Enhanced disclosure

c) Collection and communication of information

d) Risk identification and mitigation

e) Gap analyses and corrective action.

Management needs to identify procedural gaps and voids, and develop strong, cost-effective, internal controls. This section deals with identification of controls and attestation that those controls are being monitored and reported.

— — — — — — — — — — — — — — — —

4.2 *Integrity and Disclosure*

The organization will define (as applicable) processes for:

a) *Financial integrity and accurate disclosure*
b) *Key performance indicators and reporting of deviations*
c) *Management responsibilities and oversight*
d) *Safeguards (e.g., periodic inventories, reconciliations,)*
e) *Record keeping and retention*
f) *Recording and disbursement of funds*
g) *Risk analysis and mitigation*
h) *Conflicts of interests, outside interests, and related transactions*
i) *Timesheet and travel claim preparation, to include:*
1. *Time recording*
2. *Labor charging/rate determination*
3. *Customer billing*
j) *Copyrighted or licensed materials*
k) *Accurate representation of data and credentials*
l) *Reporting adverse personnel information.*

4.3 Personnel Recruitment and Selection

Personnel should be recruited into the organization in a documented manner that seeks out and attracts the following:

- Exemplary personal and community ethical standards,
- Industry-specific experience and qualifications,
- Existing and potential leadership and management skills,
- Above average corporate behavior,
- Communication and team skills, and
- Creativity and innovation.

Organizations using employment agencies must require the same documented selection standards as those directly practiced by the organization.

4.3 Personnel Recruitment and Selection

The organization will develop ethically responsible procedures for the recruitment and selection of personnel so as to positively influence and reinforce company culture. The organization will implement and maintain the following as applicable:

    a) *A policy statement precluding discrimination on grounds of ethnic origin, handicap or gender or other discrimination,*

    b) *A signed agreement by prospective employees adhering to the Statement of Corporate Responsibility Policy,*

    c) *A documented selection procedure for employment agencies servicing the organization,*

    d) *Criteria for evaluation of the Corporate Responsibility of employment agencies doing business with the organization,*

    e) *Recording the results of the measures.*

4.4 Contracts of Employment (if applicable)

Organizations should ensure that employees have no doubt regarding the existence of the Corporate Responsibility Management System and their requirement to state their adherence to it in writing. This is optimally performed at the signing of the contract of employment.

4.4 Contracts of Employment (If Applicable)

The organization will reflect the Code of Ethics and Standards of Conduct in its employment contracts for both full-time and part-time employees.

4.5 Performance Review

Management should ensure that ethical behavior in general and conformance with the Corporate Responsibility Management System in particular are reflected in periodic and special performance evaluations.

4.5 Performance Review

Management will ensure that scheduled personnel performance reviews cover adherence to the policies and practices of the Corporate Responsibility System. Specifically:

a) *The organization will describe the procedures for carrying out the above-mentioned appraisal / performance discussion, in its regulations.*

b) *Discussion will cover all areas and issues that can affect the work and the performance of the employee.*

c) *The employee to be appraised must be informed about what is required of him or her in the function that he or she is carrying out.*

d) *The organization will produce a standard appraisal form for use by reporting seniors in the organization, and*

e) *An appeals procedure.*

4.6 Requirements for Suppliers/Subcontractors

The organization should establish documented processes to identify ethically responsible suppliers (including subcontractors) for purchased products or services and to routinely re-evaluate their continued performance, to include:

- Evaluation of competence,
- Performance against competitors,
- Contract adherence and quality of performance,
- Awareness of the organization's Corporate Responsibility management system.

Note: Clause 7.4.2: *Supplier Control Process* in the ISO 9000 International Standard provides supplier quality standards. Adherence to those standards should ensure ethical performance of suppliers.

4.6 Requirements for Suppliers/Subcontractors

The organization will ensure that suppliers are aware of the applicable sections of the Code of Ethics and Standards of Conduct and the expectations of suppliers in accordance with it. Subcontractors are considered suppliers for the purposes of this Standard.

4.7 Community Responsibility

The organization must fully define its roles, responsibilities, and authorities as a member of the community, to include:

- Identification of environmental aspects of operation,
- Assignment of monitoring duties to a management representative,
- Periodically evaluating performance of community responsibilities as part of the Management Involvement process,
- Execution of policies and objectives,
- Development of recommendations for improvement and appropriate feedback mechanisms, and
- Normal and emergency lines of communication.

--- --- --- --- --- --- --- --- --- --- --- --- ---

4.7 Community Responsibility

The organization will develop a policy defining its responsibility to the community (i.e., district, town/city, and state/region).

4.8 Quality of Life

Management should recognize its impact (positive or negative) on the quality of life of its personnel and identify and allocate resources as necessary. This can include:

- An initial benchmarking, as with a climate survey,
- Open meetings and communication, and
- Assessing the impact of other nonconformities in terms of personnel and community quality of life and including those assessments in management reviews.

--- --- --- --- --- --- --- --- --- --- --- --- ---

4.8 Quality of Life

The organization will monitor its effect on the quality of life of:

- *a) Employees and their families,*
- *b) The geographical area in which it operates and has potential to impact positively or negatively.*

4.9 Competition

A Corporate Responsibility Management System should address the importance of fair and appropriate competition in the marketplace, in accordance with

- Applicable statutory and regulatory requirements, and
- The organization's standards of honesty and fairness.

4.9 Competition

The organization will conform to applicable statutory and regulatory requirements with regard to:

a) *The development and maintenance of pricing structures,*

b) *Delivery terms and conditions,*

c) *Exclusion of supply to particular customers,*

d) *The use of different prices for the same level of performance.*

e) *Doing business with organizations that use restrictive competitive practices,*

f) *The fixing of prices,*

g) *Dividing of markets, and*

h) *Restrictive production or supply practice.*

4.10 Accident Reporting

Ethical operation means that accidents, environmental incidents, or other unsafe conditions are reported in an open, expedient manner, in accordance with a documented procedure and without fear of potential legal ramifications or personal reprisal.

4.10 Accident Reporting

The organization will develop procedures for expeditiously reporting safety or environmental accidents to proper authorities.

4.11 Hazardous Material Control and Management

Organizations that produce or consume hazardous materials in their processes must develop and maintain a scrupulously effective program of hazardous material control and management, to include:

- Identification of all hazardous materials involved or produced in the organization,
- Required handling and spill prevention and mitigation,
- Accident reporting
- Routine and first responder training
- Certifications as appropriate.

4.11 Hazardous Materials

The organization will develop (as applicable) procedures to prevent or reduce the environmental risks related to the storage, transfer, and transport of dangerous materials, to include:

a) *National laws and regulations, guidelines, decisions, and permits,*
b) *Responsibilities for carrying out formulated policy,*
c) *Procedures for the storage, transfer and transport of dangerous materials,*
d) *Training and qualifications of users.*

4.12 Pollution Prevention

Organizations should develop and implement processes and practices to avoid or minimize the creation, emission, or discharge of any type of pollutant or waste, in order to preclude adverse impacts on the environment.

4.12 Pollution Prevention

The organization will develop (as applicable) pollution prevention procedures to include (as applicable):

a) *Identification of all potential sources of pollution, wastes, and emissions,*

b) *Identification of all applicable statutory and regulatory requirements.*
c) *Reduction measures*
d) *Recycling opportunities.*

The organization will discuss the operation of the pollution prevention procedures at scheduled Oversight Reviews and record discussions, nonconformities, and corrective and preventive actions.

4.13 Energy Conservation

It makes moral as well as economic sense for organizations to develop and implement documented energy conservation programs. Conservation and recycling programs are responsible organizational and community actions and improve bottom profitability through cost avoidance.

4.13 Energy Conservation

The organization will develop an Energy Conservation Program, to include (as applicable):

a) *An energy conservation policy,*
b) *A survey identifying all sources of energy expenditure and the technical and economic feasibility of implementing specific energy conservation measures.*
c) *Periodic evaluation of the system during the internal audits and management reviews.*

4.14 Environmental Assessment

An organization implementing a Corporate Responsibility Management System and not yet having an environmental management system should benchmark its initial position relative to environmental compliance. It can effectively do this by conducting (or causing the conduct of) an assessment of its environmental compliance status with regard to:

- Hazardous material control and management
- Its activities and processes,
- Applicable statutory and regulatory requirements,
- Recycling and energy conservation,
- Supplier selection,
- Contract development,
- Development of environmental aspects.

4.14 Environmental Assessment

As applicable, the organization will carry out, or have carried out a survey into the environmental aspects of the activities, and into alternatives for those activities which constitute a potential burden on the environment.

4.14.1 Environmental Aspects

The organization will identify all relevant environmental aspects of products and services, to include (as applicable):

a) *A purchasing policy reflecting for products and services with potential environmental impact,*
b) *Criteria and selection of the most suitable suppliers.*

4.15 Competence, Experience, and Training

Management should ensure that the necessary competence, experience, and training are available for the effective and efficient operation of the organization. Management should consider analysis of both the present and expected competence needs as compared to the competence already existing in the organization.

4.15 Competence, Experience, and Training

The organization will establish requirements with regard to the education and instruction of all personnel and, in addition, will set standards for competence, experience, and training in the following areas related to the Corporate Responsibility Management System:

a) *Occupational Safety and Health*
b) *Energy conservation*
c) *Hazardous Material Control and Management*
d) *Pollution prevention*
e) *Recycling*
f) *Contracting*
g) *Procurement*
h) *Internal auditing, and*
i) *Finance and accounting.*

4.16 Risk Assessment and Minimization

Risk assessment and minimization is currently recommended in the ISO 14000 International Environmental Management Systems Standard, to evaluate and quantify (albeit subjectively) the environmental aspects of organizations and their potential impacts on the organization and the community.

Organizations will always be limited in the resources available to them and will need to identify their most likely problems, in order to prioritize those limited resources most effectively. Organizations should develop and use structured risk assessment, minimization, and management processes. This means assigning numerical values to probable outcomes of the different processes performed by the organization, the probability of consequence occurrence, and gravity of the consequences. Structuring like this creates risk "matrices".

Organizations can and should develop these risk matrices to evaluate potential ethical as well as environmental outcomes of different courses of action.

--- --- --- --- --- --- --- --- --- --- --- ---

4.16 Risk Assessment and Minimization

The organization will implement risk assessment and minimization procedures for all activities and components in order to:

a) *Determine a relative ranking of potential risks, and determine the likely frequencies and consequences of those risks*
b) *Recognize opportunities as well as risks, and*
c) *Formalize and document knowledge for more precise decision-making.*

4.17 Emergency Preparedness and Response

Organizations have an ethical responsibility to ensure not only that facilities and working conditions contain a minimum of safety hazards but also that documented plans exist to preclude or minimize the effects of on-site emergencies, such as fires.

Moreover, organizations should ensure preparedness and response plans are adequate, though a structured program of periodic training and drills and exercises.

— — — — — — — — — — — — — — — —

4.17 Emergency Preparedness and Response

The organization will develop an emergency response plan covering (as applicable):

a) *Identification of potential disasters or emergencies in the organization*
b) *Preplanned responses*
c) *Emergency evacuation, aid, and assistance*
d) *Safeguarding organization personnel*
e) *Consequence management (including drills or exercises)*
f) *Disaster prevention*
g) *Cooperation with external aid and assistance organizations*
h) *Employee awareness training*
i) *Emergency reporting*
j) *Business continuity.*

4.18 Absence Due to Illness

Organizations should realize that significant safety or morale problems in the workplace may result in absenteeism. Accordingly, management should monitor absenteeism as a potential symptom of underlying root causes.

— — — — — — — — — — — — — — — —

4.18 Absence Due to Illness

The organization will develop and implement procedures to reduce work related absenteeism and incapacity through illness, to include:

a) The definition of work related absenteeism and incapacity through illness
b) Information and training for managers regarding absenteeism, and ways to address employee illness, absence, and return,
c) Maintenance of absenteeism statistics, and
d) Work related health investigation.

4.19 Safety and Health

Organizations whose management shows genuine and proactive concern for the safety and health of the assigned personnel routinely enjoy higher morale and productivity. Absenteeism diminishes, as do work-related sickness and accidents. However, organizations do have economic and legal requirements to develop and implement effective safety and health programs.

— — — — — — — — — — — — — — — — —

4.19 Safety and Health

The organization will develop and implement a safety and health promotion policy, to include (as applicable):
a) Occupational safety
b) Accident prevention and safe human behavior
c) Workplace cleanliness and sanitation (including ventilation systems)
d) Exercise and nutrition
e) Transportation safety.

4.20 Working hours

Organizations need to formally develop and state policies regarding working on and off-site working hours and the types of activities to be engaged in during those periods. Standard working hours should be appropriate for the activities of the organization and in agreement with statutory and regulatory requirements and limitations.

— — — — — — — — — — — — — — — — —

1.20 Working hours

The organization will develop and implement policies regarding working hours, to include (as applicable):

a) *Applicable statutory and regulatory requirements*
b) *Core working hours*
c) *Employee categories*
d) *Emergency recalls*
e) *Working from home*
f) *Overtime, and*
g) *Project time and billing (if appropriate).*

---

5. METRICS ESTABLISHMENT

Just as with quality and environmental management systems, management should ensure that corporate responsibility management systems contain the means to measure and analyze ethical performance within the organization, identify deficiencies, and identify "actionable" improvements. Examples of methods from which shortcomings can be identified and remedied include:

- Satisfaction surveys
- Internal reviews
- Organizational metrics (described herein)
- Self-assessment.

Management should ensure the establishment of an effective and efficient internal review process to assess the strengths and weaknesses of the System. The process provides an independent tool for obtaining objective evidence about the operation of the organization.

Management should also consider establishment of self-assessment mechanisms to supplement audit evidence regarding the Corporate Responsibility Management System.

5.1 General

The organization will establish and maintain documented procedures to monitor and measure, on a regular basis, the key characteristics of its operations and activities that can have significant impact on the professional and business responsibilities of the organization.

5.1.1 Personnel, Customer, and Stakeholder Satisfaction

The organization will periodically measure personnel, board, and stakeholders' satisfaction, to include:

   a) *Effectiveness of the Corporate Responsibility System,*
   b) *Effectiveness of the Code of Ethics and Standards of Conduct,*
   c) *Personnel, customer, and stakeholder feedback.*

5.1.2 Internal reviews/Audits

At least once per year, the organization will review the effectiveness of the Corporate Responsibility Management System, to determine:

   a) *Determine whether or not the Corporate Responsibility System:*
      1) *Conforms to the organization's requirements and to statutory and regulatory requirements*
      2) *Has been properly implemented and maintained*
   b) *Provide information on the results to management.*

5.2 Nonconformance and Corrective and Preventive Action

The organization will establish and maintain procedures for defining authority, responsibility, and accountability for ethical nonconformities, taking action to mitigate any impacts caused and for initiating and completing corrective and preventive action.

Corrective or preventive actions taken to eliminate the causes of actual of potential nonconformities will be appropriate for the magnitude of the problem and commensurate with actual or potential impact.

— — — — — — — — — — — — — — — —

5.2 Nonconformance and Corrective and Preventive Action

The organization will establish and maintain procedures for resolving nonconformities to the System, and take action to resolve any negative impacts by initiating and completing corrective and/or preventive action.

5.3 Continual Improvement

Management should create a culture of continual improvement, to sensitize employees to the importance of ever-higher standards of ethical conduct and encourages them to seek opportunities to improve ethical performance. Management can achieve and maintain a state of continual improvement by:

- Setting objectives within the organization,
- Benchmarking own and competitor performance,
- Recognition and reward for achievement of improvements, and
- Including suppliers in the improvement processes.

— — — — — — — — — — — — — — — —

5.3 Continual Improvement

The organization will continually improve the effectiveness of the Corporate Responsibility System by using policy, objectives, findings and analyses, research into personnel, customer, and stakeholders' satisfaction, corrective and preventive measures, and management oversight, ensuring that timely measures are taken.

Chart 1. Establishing a Corporate Responsibility Management System

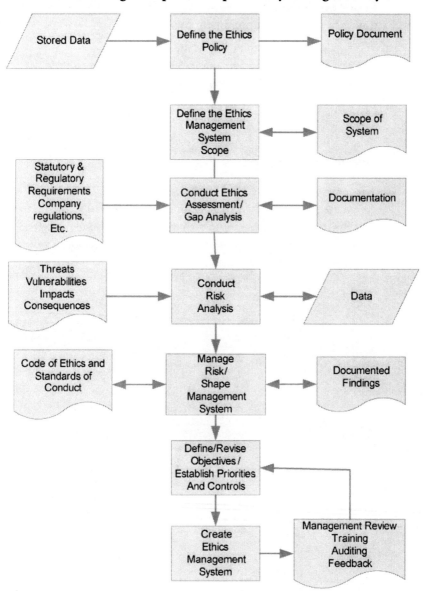

Appendix One:
Glossary

For purposes of this book and the MVO 8000 Standard, the following definitions apply.

Accountability

The acceptance of recognition from another party (e.g., a superior or supervisor) for the success or failure of an objective

Audit

A systematic and independent survey to determine whether or not activities carried out in the area of company ethics, and the corresponding results achieved, conform with statutory and regulatory requirements, have been implemented effectively, and are appropriate to achieving the objectives.

Auditor

A person who is qualified to carry out audits

Authority

The right of an individual to make the necessary decisions or take the necessary action to achieve established goals and objectives

Code of Ethics and Standards of Conduct

The implemented ethical practices within the organization, in compliance with both internal and statutory and regulatory requirements, reflecting feedback from customers, regulators, and the community

Business Ethics

Ethics applicable to business-customer relationships, requiring that businesses act in the interests of the customer (See Professional Ethics).

Continual Improvement (of the Corporate Responsibility Management System)

The process of ongoing enhancement in order to achieve improvements in overall performance in line with the organization's ethical policy

Corrective Action

Action taken to correct a problem or nonconformance to a policy or procedure

Effectiveness

The extent to which planned activities are carried out, and the planned results achieved.

Efficiency

The relationship between the results achieved and the resources used

Environment

Surroundings in which an organization operates, including air, water, land, natural resources, humans, and their interrelation.

Environmental Aspect

An environmental aspect (as defined in ISO 14001) is "an element of the organization's activities, products, and/or services that which can interact with the environment."

Environmental Impact

An environmental impact (as defined in ISO 14001) is "any change to the environment, whether adverse or beneficial wholly or partially resulting from an organization's activities, products, or services."

Ethics

The science concerned with systematic reflection on rules and issues. The way in which people act, and the rules that form the basis of these actions.

Ethics Management Planning

The aspect of ethics management related to determining the objectives and specifying the necessary operational processes and related resources required to satisfy the ethics objectives.

Corporate Responsibility System

The established, documented, and implemented system that directs and controls the ethical functioning of the organization

Ethics Objectives

Measurable achievements sought after by the organization in pursuit of stated ethics policies.

Ethics Policy

The stated overall intention and direction of the organization with regard to ethics and ethical conduct

Feedback

Communication (in whatever form) that management receives regarding some action that it is about to take or has already taken; an indispensable part of the decision-making process.

Follow-up

Checking on the success or failure of a process implemented or changed, an order given, or some other modification done with the object of improving a process, product, or service.

Interested party

Individual or group within or affected by the performance of an organization

Management

Personnel at the highest level charged with and responsible for coordinated activities to direct and control the organization

Nonconformity

Findings or conditions that do not satisfy the specified requirements

Organization

A company, corporation, firm, enterprise, authority, or institution, or part or combination thereof, whether incorporated or not, public or private, that has its own functions and administration.

Pollution Prevention

The use of processes, practices, materials, or products that avoid, reduce, or control pollution, which may include recycling, treatment, process changes, control mechanisms, efficient use of resources and material substitution.

Preventive Action

A measure that is taken to eliminate the cause of, and prevent the occurrence of, a <u>potential</u> irregularity, deficiency or other undesirable situation

Process Approach

The identification and management of several linked activities and associated human resources. With regard to a structured Corporate Responsibility System, the process approach emphasizes the importance of:

a) Understanding and operating in accordance with established rules of conduct,
b) The need to consider the process in terms of added value,
c) Monitoring results of process performance and effectiveness, and
d) Continual improvement of processes based on objective measurement.

Procedure

A specified way to perform an activity

Professional Ethics

Ethics that are applicable to all professional-client relationships, requiring that professionals act only in the interests of the client (See Business Ethics)

Responsibility

The assignment for completion of objectives

Responsible Business Practice

The carrying out business on the basis of standards and values, whereby business is carried out for own interests but also for what is good for people, the environment and society.

Statutory and Regulatory Requirements

Obligations that stem from legislation, regulations, rules, codes, statutes, and other impositions

Supplier

The provider (producer, subsidiary, sub-contractor, importer) of products and services in a contractual situation

Stakeholders

All parties that have an interest in the performance of an organization (e.g., board, investors, commissioners, employees, local government, and the community).

Work Environment

The conditions under which work is performed in the organization, including facilities, equipment, and services. Work environment can also include physical, psychological, and environmental factors, such as temperature, ergonomics, and atmospheric composition.

Appendix Two—
Corporate Responsibility Management
System Review Checklist

1. CORPORATE RESPONSIBILITY SYSTEM REQUIREMENTS

1.1 General

Has the organization developed, documented, and implemented a Corporate Responsibility Management System (CRMS) that will:

o   Identify all processes and interactions
o   Determine the interaction between these various processes and interactions,
o   Determine the (ethics-based) effectiveness criteria for the implementation and monitoring of these processes,
o   Show the availability of resources and information relevant to the processes,
o   Monitor, measure, and analyze the processes
o   Take necessary actions to:
  •   Achieve the planned objectives,
  •   Implement corrective and preventive action, and
  •   Continuously improve the processes?

1.1 Policy and Procedural Requirements

1.1.1 General

Does the CRMS include a manual, containing documented explanations of policies and objectives, and procedures required by this International Standard?

1.2.2 Corporate Responsibility Management System Manual

Does the organization maintain an Corporate Responsibility Management System manual that includes:

o   The scope of the Corporate Responsibility Management System,
o   The documented procedures established for the system or

reference to them, and

- o A description of the interaction between the processes of the Corporate Responsibility Management System.

2. MANAGEMENT INVOLVEMENT

1.1 Involvement of Management

Does management demonstrate its social and ethical involvement with society, the governing board, other stakeholders, and own personnel by:

- o Developing, implementing, and continuously improving the Corporate Responsibility Management System,
- o Communicating to all levels in the organization the importance of satisfying the requirements, standards, and values used by the organization to carry out its business,
- o Communicating to all levels in the organization the importance of satisfying statutory and regulatory requirements in the practice of company ethics,
- o Developing and implementing the company's ethics policies and objectives,
- o Carrying out a program or internal audits, and
- o Making resources available?

2.2 Corporate Responsibility Management Policy

Has management determined a policy and ensured that the policy:

- o Is suitable and consistent with the needs of the organization,
- o Is consistent with statutory and regulatory requirements,
- o Provides for continuous improvement of the CRMS
- o Provides the framework for development of measurable objectives,
- o Is communicated to, and understood by, the whole organization,
- o Is periodically assessed for its suitability?

2.3 Administration and Management

Has management ensured that all responsibilities and authorities are documented and communicated through the organization, be establishing:

- o The tasks, responsibilities, and authorities of all employees with respect to carrying out the formulated ethics policy.
- o The tasks, responsibilities, and authorities of assigned supporting contractors, as applicable?

2.3.1 Oversight Officer/Management Representative

Has management appointed an oversight officer/management representative, who will be responsible for the development, implementation, and maintenance of the Corporate Responsibility Management System?

Does the Management Representative work directly for the President and periodically report on the performance of the Corporate Responsibility Management System and identify potential improvements?

1.1.2 Internal Communication

Has management provided a structure to inform personnel about the Corporate Responsibility Management System, in which ethics management is regularly reviewed within the organization and communication takes place at all levels and functions regarding the effectiveness of the Corporate Responsibility Management System?

2.4 Management Oversight

Does management periodically review the effectiveness of the Corporate Responsibility Management System?

During each review, does management determine:
- o If the Corporate Responsibility Management System has to be modified,
- o If policies have to be modified, or objectives amended,
- o The need for (or status of) corrective and corrective actions?

3 HUMAN RESOURCES

3.1 General

Are personnel trained on the Corporate Responsibility Management System and how it applies to their positions and functions?

3.1.2 Ethics Awareness Training

Has management:

o   Developed and scheduled ethics awareness training for all personnel,

o   Evaluated and measured the effectiveness of the training, and

o   Recorded all relevant training conducted?

1.1.2 Complaints Procedure

Has management provided employees with a process for communicating instances of unacceptable behavior, to include:

o   The complaint submission procedure

o   Responsibilities for complaints procedure administration,

o   Confidentiality of complaints

o   Appeal rights of personnel accused?

3.1.4 Personnel Representation

Has management created a consultative body within the organization:

o   To monitor the ethical functioning of the organization and the interests of all the employees,

o   To define objectives, tasks, responsibilities, authorities, and procedures in the operation of the Corporate Responsibility Management System,

o   To review instances of reported violations of the Corporate Responsibility Management System, and

o   To administer the organization's system of sanctions (see 6.3)?

3.2 Sanctions

Has management developed a system of sanctions to include:

o   Definition and description undesirable ethical behavior in the organization,

o   The manner in which unacceptable ethical conduct is reported,

o   The manner in which corrective action will be taken, and

o   The manner in which personal information is documented and recorded?

3.3 Code of Ethics and Standards of Conduct.

Has management created a *Code of Ethics and Standards of Conduct*, to include:

- o The Corporate Responsibility Management System,
- o Statutory and regulatory requirements,
- o Formal standards of performance and expectations,
- o The organization's moral values with respect to personnel, customers, competitors, suppliers, and society,
- o Unacceptable ethical behavior as it applies to the organization,
- o Legal obligations of the organization and its members,
- o Intellectual property,
- o Physical and environmental security,
- o Access control,
- o Communications and operations management,
- o Use of company property,
- o Internet usage,
- o Timesheet and travel claim preparation,
- o Working from home,
- o Internal auditing processes?

4 MANAGING THE CORPORATE RESPONSIBILITY MANAGEMENT SYSTEM

4.1 Communication and Participation

Does management involve all levels of the organization in the operation of the Corporate Responsibility Management System?

- o Do committees will ensure that meetings are recorded, and
- o Is sufficient time and resources are allocated?

4.2 Integrity and Disclosure

Has the organization will defined (as applicable) processes for:

- o Financial integrity and accurate disclosure
- o Key performance indicators and reporting of deviations
- o Management responsibilities and oversight
- o Safeguards (e.g., periodic inventories, reconciliations,)
- o Record keeping and retention
- o Recording and disbursement of funds

o   Risk analysis and mitigation
o   Conflicts of interests, outside interests, and related transactions
o   Timesheet and travel claim preparation, to include:
o   Time recording
o   Labor charging/rate determination
o   Customer billing
o   Copyrighted or licensed materials
o   Accurate representation of data and credentials
o   Reporting adverse personnel information.

4.3   Personnel Recruitment and Selection

Has the organization developed ethically responsible procedures for the recruitment and selection of personnel so as to positively influence and reinforce company culture?

Has the organization maintained the following as applicable:

o   A policy statement precluding discrimination on grounds of ethnic origin, handicap or gender or other discrimination,
o   A signed agreement by prospective employees adhering to the Statement of Ethics Policy,
o   A documented selection procedure for employment agencies servicing the organization,
o   Criteria for evaluation of the ethics of employment agencies doing business with the organization,
o   Recording the results of the measures?

4.4   Contracts of Employment

Does the organization reflect the *Code of Ethics and Standards of Conduct* in its employment contracts?

4.5   Performance Review

Does management ensure that scheduled personnel performance reviews cover adherence to the policies and practices of the Corporate Responsibility Management System? Specifically:

o   Does the organization describe the procedures for carrying out the above-mentioned appraisal/performance?
o   Does discussion cover all areas and issues that can affect the work and the performance of the employee?
o   Are employees to be appraised informed about what is

required of them in the function that they are carrying out?

- o   Does the organization have a standard appraisal form for use by reporting seniors in the organization?
- o   Is there an appeals procedure?

4.6   Requirements for Suppliers

Does the organization ensure that suppliers are aware of the applicable sections of the *Code of Ethics and Standards of Conduct* and the expectations of suppliers in accordance with the *Code of Ethics and Standards of Conduct?*

4.7   Community Responsibility

Is there a policy defining the organization's responsibility to the community (i.e., district, town/city, and region)?

4.8   Quality of Life

Does the organization monitor its effect on the quality of life of:

- o   Employees and their families,
- o   Major suppliers and subcontractors
- o   The geographical area in which it operates and has potential to impact positively or negatively?

4.9   Competition

Does the organization conform to applicable statutory and regulatory requirements with regard to:

- o   The development and maintenance of pricing structures
- o   Delivery terms and conditions
- o   Exclusion of supply to particular customers
- o   The use of different prices for the same level of performance
- o   Doing business with organizations that use restrictive competitive practices
- o   The fixing of prices
- o   Dividing of markets
- o   Restrictive production or supply practices?

4.10 Accident Reporting

Has the organization developed procedures for directly reporting safety or environmental accidents to proper authority?

4.11 Hazardous Materials

Has the organization will developed (as applicable) procedures to prevent or reduce the environmental risks related to the storage, transfer and transport of dangerous materials? Specifically:

o Adherence to National laws and regulations, guidelines, decisions, and permits,

o Responsibilities for carrying out formulated policy,

o Procedures for the storage, transfer and transport of dangerous materials,

o Training and qualifications of users?

4.12 Pollution Prevention

Has the organization developed (as applicable) pollution prevention procedures to include:

o Identification of all potential sources of pollution, wastes, and emissions,

o Identification of all applicable statutory and regulatory requirements.

o Reduction measures

o Recycling opportunities?

Does the organization discuss the operation of the pollution prevention procedures at scheduled Management Reviews and record discussions, nonconformities, and corrective and preventive actions?

4.13 Energy Conservation

Has the organization developed an Energy Conservation Program, to include:

o An energy conservation policy,

o Recognition of all applicable environmental laws and regulations and the conditions that are stipulated in the environmental license as applicable),

o A survey identifying all sources of energy expenditure and the technical and economic feasibility of implementing specific energy conservation measures.

o Periodic evaluation of the system during the internal audits and management reviews?

4.14 Environmental Assessment

Does the organization carry out, or have carried out a survey into the environmental aspects of the activities, and into alternatives for those activities which constitute a potential burden on the environment?

4.14.1 Environmental Aspects

Has the organization identified all relevant environmental aspects of products and services, to include:

o   A purchasing policy reflecting for products and services with potential environmental impact,

o   Criteria and selection of the most suitable suppliers?

4.15 Competence, Experience, and Training

Has the organization established requirements with regard to the education and instruction of all personnel and set standards for competence, experience, and training in the following areas related to the Corporate Responsibility Management System. Specifically:

o   Occupational Safety and Health,

o   Energy conservation

o   Hazardous Material Control and Management

o   Pollution prevention, and

o   Recycling.

o   Contracting,

o   Procurement,

o   Internal auditing, and

o   Finance and accounting?

4.16 Risk Assessment and Minimization

Has the organization implemented risk assessment and minimization procedures for all activities and components, in order to:

o   Determine a relative ranking of potential risks, and determine the likely frequencies and consequences of those risks,

o   Recognize opportunities as well as risks, and

o   Formalize and document knowledge for more precise decision-making?

4.17 Emergency Preparedness and Response

Has the organization developed an emergency response plan covering:

- o Identification of potential disasters or emergencies in the organization
- o Preplanned responses
- o Emergency evacuation, aid, and assistance,
- o Safeguarding organization personnel
- o Consequence management (including drills or exercises)
- o Disaster prevention,
- o Cooperation with external aid and assistance organizations
- o Employee awareness training
- o Emergency reporting?

4.18 Absence Due to Illness

Does the organization have documented procedures with regard to work related absenteeism and incapacity through illness, to include:

- o The definition of work related absenteeism and incapacity through illness.
- o Social and medical counseling of employees who are ill or incapacitated. or who are returning to the workplace,
- o Information and training for managers regarding absenteeism, and ways to address employee illness, absence, and return,
- o Maintenance of absenteeism statistics, and
- o Work related health investigation?

4.19 Safety and Health

Does the organization have a published safety and health promotion policy, to include:

- o Occupational safety,
- o Accident prevention and safe human behavior,
- o Workplace cleanliness and sanitation (including ventilation systems),
- o Exercise and nutrition,
- o Transportation safety?

4.20 Working hours

Does the organization have written policies regarding working hours, to include:

- o   Applicable statutory and regulatory requirements,
- o   Core working hours,
- o   Employee categories,
- o   Emergency recalls,
- o   Working from home,
- o   Overtime, and
- o   Charge number usage (if appropriate)?

5.   METRICS ESTABLISHMENT

5.1   General

Does the organization have documented procedures to monitor and measure the key characteristics of its operations and activities that can have significant impact on the professional and business ethics of the organization?

5.1.1 Personnel, Customer, and Stakeholder Satisfaction

Does the organization have a research methodology for periodic measurement of personnel, board, and stakeholders' satisfaction, to include:

- o   Effectiveness of the Corporate Responsibility Management System,
- o   Effectiveness of the Code of Ethics and Standards of Conduct,
- o   Personnel, customer, and stakeholder feedback?

5.1.2 Internal Reviews/Audits

Does the organization will conduct periodic internal reviews/audits to determine the effectiveness of the Corporate Responsibility Management System, in order to:

- o   Determine whether or not the Corporate Responsibility Management System conforms to the organization's requirements and to statutory and regulatory requirements

Has the internal audit system been properly implemented and maintained?

Are the results of reviews provided to management?

5.2 Nonconformance and Corrective and Preventive Action

Does the organization have procedures for defining responsibility and authority for ethical nonconformities, taking action to mitigate any impacts caused and for initiating and completing corrective and preventive action?

Are corrective or preventive actions taken to eliminate the cause of actual or potential nonconformities appropriate for the magnitude of the problem and commensurate with actual or potential impact?

3   Continual Improvement

Does the organization continually improve the effectiveness of the Corporate Responsibility Management System by using policy, objectives, audit results, data analysis, research into personnel, customer, and stakeholders' satisfaction, corrective and preventive measures, and management review meetings?

When shortcomings are detected from audit results, data analyses, satisfaction surveys, or management reviews, does the organization ensure that timely corrective and preventive measures are taken?

Is the effectiveness of measures taken documented?

NOTES:

Appendix Three—
SARBANES-OXLEY ATTESTATION CHECKLIST

	Yes	No
Integrity, ethical values, and behavior of key executives		
Is there a widely communicated statement of values or other code of conduct that is evident in management's words and actions?		
Do rewards and incentives support an appropriate ethical tone at the company?		
Is there evidence that management disciplines departures from proper conduct?		
Management's control consciousness and operating style		
Is there effective oversight by the board of directors, and is the structure appropriate?		
Are financial reporting policies conservative?		
Do regular communications support the importance of internal controls?		
Does management dedicate enough time and resources to internal control assessment and quickly address deficiencies?		
Are financial and other targets realistic, and are incentives balanced?		
Commitment to competence		
Is departmental staffing adequate, and are employees properly prepared for their assigned level of responsibility?		
Is management's functional experience broad, and not overly reliant on one or two individuals?		
Board of Directors' participation in governance and oversight		
Is there sufficient independent representation on the board, as evidenced by diverse backgrounds and expertise, no ties to the company other than the director, as well as active and significant participation in company matters?		
Does the board determine the compensation of executive officers and chief internal auditor?		
Is the audit committee independent and vigilant, and does it include at least one financial expert and have the authority and resources to discharge its responsibilities?		

	Yes	No
Does the audit committee maintain a direct line of communication with internal and external auditors?		
Organizational structure, operating style, and assignment of authority and responsibility:		
Is the organizational structure appropriate for the size of the company, and does it support the flow of required management information required to run the organization?		
Are the responsibilities of individual managers clearly defined?		
Is there adequate supervision of decentralized operations?		
Is there excessive turnover in key functions such as accounting, data processing, and internal audit?		
Is there a structure for assigning ownership of accounts, applications, and databases?		
Human resources policies and procedures:		
Are there written policies and procedures covering hiring, training, promoting, compensating, and terminating employees? Are they clear, current, and communicated regularly?		
Are there written job descriptions or other methods to inform personnel of their duties?		
Is performance periodically evaluated?		
Risk Assessment		
Objective setting:		
Is the strategic plan communicated in such a way that all employees have an understanding of the company's strategy? Are company-specific objectives established, communicated, monitored, and consistent with strategy?		

	Yes	No
Are relevant, measurable process-level objectives for all major business processes, including information technology?		
Are all levels of management involved in the objective-setting process?		
Risk analysis and mitigation:		
Is a risk assessment regularly performed for entity and process objectives for both external and internal sources? Does the board of directors address significant risks identified?		
Is there a new product/business committee or approval process that evaluates proposals against objectives and adequately assesses all relevant risks? Are significant initiatives board-approved?		
Are privacy and data protection policies in place and operational?		
Does internal audit perform a periodic risk analysis? Are actions taken to address these risks?		
Managing change:		
Are contingency plans maintained for changes in market conditions, capacity constraints, business disruptions, or access to the financial markets?		
Are budgets and forecasts used to identify significant changes in the operating environment?		
Are there individuals or groups responsible for updating management regarding changes in accounting standards, legislation, workforce pool, market demographics or spending patterns, competitor movements, foreign political risk, and so on?		
Do new systems and process initiatives go through change control systems?		

	Yes	No
If restructuring a business, department or process, are the effects on the other businesses and accounting department evaluated? Are transferred or terminated employees' control responsibilities reassigned? Are safeguards implemented to protect the company against disgruntled employees?		
Is there a process to ensure that changes in GAAP are properly applied? Does the board of directors review and approve changes to accounting policies?		
Control Activities		
Policies and procedures:		
Are policies and procedures periodically evaluated (at least annually) and updated? Is clear ownership assigned for this evaluation at an appropriate level of management?		
Are accounting and closing procedures followed consistently throughout the year? Are transactions booked in a timely fashion and properly documented?		
Does an appropriate level of senior management review significant accounting estimates and supporting documentation for topside journal entries and unusual or non-routine transactions?		
Is there a process to ensure that changes in GAAP are properly applied? Does the board of directors review and approve changes to accounting policies?		
Monitor objectives:		
Does management regularly monitor key performance indicators? Are variances from expected performance investigated and resolved?		
Are deviations from expected performance discussed with the board of directors at least every quarter?		
Are financial reports disseminated to management, together with analysis of their performance?		

	Yes	No
Organizational structure:		
Do organization charts exist?		
Are key functions segregated, such as record-keeping from asset custody, application and system programmers from IT operations, and database management, and information risk management oversight from other IT functions?		
Are appropriate approvals required to allow or adjust individual access profiles for applications, systems and databases?		
Is there a process requiring system owners to periodically and confirm access privileges?		
Safeguards:		
Are there procedures to periodically conduct physical counts to reconcile assets such as securities, inventories, property and equipment, against the accounting records, and to make proper adjustments? Are recurring adjustments investigated?		
Are liquid and valuable assets such as cash and securities regularly reconciled to the accounting records?		
Is there a document destruction policy that protects against unauthorized access to, or destruction of, records, including electronic files?		
Are key documents, such as blank checks, properly restricted and secured?		
System security:		
Are appropriate access safeguards in place to monitor and protect against unauthorized access to applications, operating systems, and databases, both from internal and external threats?		
Is there a dedicated individual or department responsible for monitoring the IT environment? Are incidents logged and investigated, and is action taken to prevent recurrence?		

	Yes	No
Are the data center and other locations (such as telecommunications closets) where important technology systems are kept, properly secured?		
Are the general IT controls periodically reviewed by internal audit or a service provider, and are results communicated to the audit committee?		
Information and Communication		
Required information:		
Can the entity currently meet, or is it developing, the capability to meet the new accelerated reporting deadlines for filing timely, accurate, reports?		
Does the board of directors receive timely information in the right amount of detail needed to discharge its responsibilities?		
Are goals, objectives, and key performance indicators measurable, and is actual performance communicated to the board of directors?		
Are procedures in place to obtain and report relevant external information, such as regulatory developments, competitor initiatives, market conditions, foreign political risks, etc.?		
Is the board of directors satisfied with the timeliness, quantity, and quality of the information received?		
Do managers have the information they need to carry out their responsibilities?		
Strategic IT development:		
Is there a technology strategy that supports business objectives and strategies?		

	Yes	No
Are policies and procedures in place to control the development, modification, conversion, or replacement of accounting and other systems? Do such policies include the thorough testing of new or modified programs (including parallel processing, where possible) authorizations be obtained before they are introduced into production?		
Is financial management involved in systems development to ensure proper controls are resident?		
If applicable, are vendor processes and application controls reviewed or are transactions otherwise outsourced? Is this assessment documented and monitored?		
Is there a reasonable level of user satisfaction with the functionality of systems provided? Is the satisfaction level monitored by technology management?		
Financial and human resources:		
Are sufficient resources, with the requisite technical capabilities, provided to develop needed information systems?		
Are the board of directors and senior management involved monitoring major system projects?		
Business continuity:		
Are programs and data files regularly backed up and stored offsite?		
Is there a business continuity/disaster recovery plan that covers critical systems and procedures? Does the plan identify critical users and systems and the time required to deliver needed resources and systems?		
Are continuity plans tested at least annually and updated to reflect changing conditions?		

	Yes	No
Communication:		
Are clear lines of authority and responsibility widely communicated?		
Are internal training processes, job descriptions, and written procedures provided in sufficient detail to ensure that employees understand their duties and responsibilities and how they relate to departmental and corporate objectives?		
Is there a mechanism for employees to report unethical, illegal, or other behaviors outside of policy to the board of directors? Is the procedure communicated clearly and regularly to the entire organization? Are all such contacts logged, investigated, addressed in a timely manner?		
Are the company's ethical standards communicated extensively and routinely, internally and externally?		
Is there a process to log, investigate, and resolve complaints from customers, vendors, or other external parties? Is top management aware of the nature and volume of complaints?		
Are there established communication channels that reach all parts of the company, even in foreign countries or remote locations?		
Is there a high level of communication and cooperation between accounting and other departments?		
Monitoring		
Evaluation of internal controls:		
Are there procedures that require management to review processes to ensure that internal controls are operating as designed? Are the scope, depth, and frequency of the reviews adequate?		
Are there procedures in place to detect when controls have been overridden?		
Are there policies and procedures in place to ensure that control exceptions are addressed?		

	Yes	No
Do adequate risk management procedures exist to manage risks inherent to the business? (e.g., are there adequate standards and oversight for the credit reviews at financial institutions or position exposures at investment banks?)		
Do managers have to sign off or approve the accuracy of their financial statements, and are they responsible when there is an error?		
Internal Review/Audit:		
Is the size and experience level of the internal review function appropriate?		
Is an Annual Internal Review Plan developed and based on an assessment of risk? Is it shared with senior management and the board of directors?		
Does the reviewer report to the review committee? Are control deficiencies reported to the review committee?		
Are review personnel independent, have no operating responsibility, and have the authority to examine any and all company operations?		
Compliance:		
Do employees have to periodically acknowledge in writing compliance with the code of conduct or similar policies?		
Are signatures required to evidence critical control activities such as reconciling accounts?		

NOTES:

Appendix Four—
KEY PERFORMANCE INDICATORS

Stakeholders (especially Board members and creditors) really like it when you can quantify your operations, spotlight trouble spots and outline courses of preventive or corrective action. It is always better if you find the problem, rather than somebody on the outside. Performance indicators form a credible base for strategic and business plans.

Here are some performance indicators that executives can use to quantitatively evaluate how well their organizations are doing.

Operational metrics

    Throughput
    Throughput as a percent of capacity
    Defects as a percent of throughput
    Number of order deliveries past due
    Rush order percent
    On-time delivery percent
    Customer satisfaction rating
    Number of complaints
    Number of complaints to revenue
    Returns as a percent of units delivered
    Number of manual journal vouchers/entries per employee
    Ration of support staff to number of employees
    Days of inventory outstanding
    Inventory turns
    Market share
    Number of outstanding audit issues
    Book to bill ration
    Days sales outstanding
    Overtime percent
    Days without workplace injury
    Number of hours that production is off-line
    Personnel/material requisitions open past threshold or benchmark

Exception Reporting

Audit reports
Assets assigned to employees in excess of threshold or benchmark
Unauthorized system access attempts
General ledger accounts without assigned owners
Assets without assigned owners
Un-reconciled accounts
Inventory aged over threshold
Wires/checks issued over $ threshold
Deliveries overdue/past-due over threshold
Sales to unapproved customers
Sales to customers over established limits
Was or suspense accounts (or other accounts that should have a zero balance) that still have a balance
Unavailable materials report
Inventory count differences
Purchase orders aged over threshold
Unmatched receipts
Unsigned management representation of financial results

Financial Metrics

Cost per unit
Revenue per full time equivalent
Employee expenses headcount
Accounts receivable turnover
Write-offs as a percent of sales
Reserves as a percent of assets
Reserves as a percent of accounts receivable over 90 days past due
Budget to actual variances
Value at risk
Market value to contract value of financial interests
Un-reconciled accounts exposure
Accounts payable aging
Financial costs as a percent of revenue
Margin percent
Regulatory capital charges
Working capital

Interest coverage
Sales, general and administrative expenses as a percent of revenue
Earnings per share
Risk-adjusted return on capital
Debt/equity trend

Monitoring

Internal threat analysis of competitor control incidents
Evaluation of proposed or pending legislation effects on current operations
Periodic threat analysis of extremist groups on current operations
Camera surveillance of key areas to identify illegal activity.

Appendix Five—
CORPORATE RESPONSIBILITY
MANAGEMENT SYSTEM MANUAL

Here is a draft Corporate Responsibility Management manual upon which you can build your system. It covers all the clauses of MVO 8000. You need only to tailor it to your specific mission and organization, promulgate it, and revise it when revision is appropriate.

Manuals are never 100% correct in the first version. It is in the review and revision process that the Manual, and the guidance and direction that it contains becomes the language of the organization.

The Manual then becomes the vehicle for the corporate responsibility mindset and for continual improvement in the organization.

XXX, INC.

CORPORATE RESPONSIBILITY MANAGEMENT SYSTEM MANUAL

This Manual and the information contained therein is the property of XXX, Inc.

It must not be reproduced or otherwise disclosed without prior consent in writing from XXX, Inc.

MANUAL IDENTIFICATION

This document is a **CONTROLLED** copy.

Copy number ____ of ____

Issued to: _____

Title_____

Holders of controlled copies will be advised of any amendments or subsequent issues.

Signed: _____   Date: _____
      Management Representative

Signed: _____   Date: _____
      President

TABLE OF CONTENTS

	DESCRIPTION	PAGE	REV.
	MANUAL IDENTIFICATION		
	TABLE OF CONTENTS		
	APPROVALS AND REVISIONS		
	AMENDMENT RECORD		
	ORGANIZATION FOREWORD		
	SCOPE OF THE CORPORATE RESPONSIBILITY MANAGEMENT SYSTEM		
	ORGANIZATION PROFILE		
	MANUAL CONTROL		

Amendment Record   **Date: Oct. 2005**

Amendment to: Section: _____   Page: _____
Amendment Details:

New Issue Level: _____ Authorized & Date: _____

Amendment to: Section: _____   Page: _____
Amendment Details:

New Issue Level: _____ Authorized & Date: _____

Amendment to: Section: _____   Page: _____
Amendment Details:

New Issue Level: _____ Authorized & Date: _____

Amendment to: Section: _____   Page: _____
Amendment Details:

New Issue Level: _____ Authorized & Date: _____

ORGANIZATION FOREWORD

This Ethics Manual describes the processes used by XXX, Inc. to satisfy the requirements of its personnel, customers, and the requirements of higher authority, particularly with regard to management of ethics processes and ethical conduct.

XXX, Inc. is obliged to ensure that its Ethics Policy is understood by all its personnel, and that its procedures are implemented and maintained at all times. This Ethics Manual is in accordance with the requirements of MVO 8000:2008. The Corporate Responsibility Management System shall be periodically and systematically reviewed by management and validated by both internal and external ethics audits.

The Corporate Responsibility Management System Representative is responsible for the control of all matters pertaining to the implementation of these procedures.

The assurance of Ethics is fundamental to all work undertaken by XXX, Inc. and procedures established and practiced by all personnel at every level in the Company's structure.

SCOPE OF THE CORPORATE RESPONSIBILITY MANAGEMENT SYSTEM

XXX, Inc. offers the following services:

- ☐
- ☐
- ☐
- ☐
- ☐

APPROVED BY:

_____

President   Date

_____

Management Representative   Date

ORGANIZATION PROFILE

XXX is a worldwide provider of innovative, best-value technology solutions. This is accomplished through providing advanced systems engineering, security, intelligence support, software, simulation, interactive training and information technology solutions for domestic and international clients. XXX has approximately xxx employees, located at our headquarters in xxx, xx satellite offices, and on-government facilities around the country.

XXX, Inc. has provided customer centric solutions for the Department of Defense, Federal Agencies, Aerospace and Defense companies and 26 Foreign Governments. XXX has more than 18-years of experience in providing classified and unclassified engineering, technical support services and technical training development for DOD aircraft and surface warfare systems.

XXX, Inc. offers a full range of product and service solutions across the following functional business areas:

➤
➤
➤
➤
➤

MANUAL CONTROL

Control of this Manual rests with the Corporate Responsibility Management System Representative.

REVISION STATUS

The revision status of each page of this Manual is stated at the bottom of the page.

DISTRIBUTION CONTROL

"Uncontrolled" and "Controlled" copies of this Manual are issued.

1. Uncontrolled copies may be distributed outside the Company with the approval of the President or the Director of Ethics Management/ Management Representative. They will have no unique identity and will be marked as an uncontrolled copy and subsequently will not be updated.
2. Controlled paper copies will each have a unique number and will be assigned to an individual by name. The Management Representative controls the distribution. The distribution is limited to one paper copy in the Document Control Center.

The Master copy is maintained by the Management Representative and retained on the server in the Document Control Center.

This list may be subjected to amendment, whereupon a new issue will be distributed and recorded on the Amendment Record.

REVIEW

The Management Representative and the MVO 8000 Steering Committee will review this manual at least once per year during Management review meetings, to verify that it continues to describe the Ethics System correctly and approve proposed changes accordingly. The date of these reviews will be recorded and minutes will be kept.

CHANGES TO THE ETHICS MANUAL

Any proposed changes, additions, or alterations to this Manual must be addressed to the Corporate Responsibility Management System Representative. Should the change, addition or alteration be approved after a consultation period with other areas, then the relevant amendments will be made, recorded on the Amendment Record, and distributed according to the Distribution List.

SECTION 1: GENERAL

1.1 PROMULGATION

XXX, Inc. recognizes its corporate responsibility and has developed a documented Corporate Responsibility Management System that complies with the MVO 8000, Corporate Responsibility Management System Standard.

This Manual provides comprehensive evidence to all customers, suppliers and Company personnel of the procedures implemented to ensure that all products, services, and community interactions reflect our highest ethical standards. This Manual also governs the creation of ethics-related documents. It will be revised as necessary to reflect review and revision. It is issued on a controlled copy basis to all internal functions affected by the Corporate Responsibility Management System, as described in Distribution Control, and on an uncontrolled copy basis to customers and suppliers at the discretion of management.

The President/CEO is responsible for evaluation and approval of the exclusions. Evaluation and approval of the exclusions is normally conducted during the Management Review process. The details are explained in the Management Review Procedure.

Sections 4-8 follow the sectional organization of the MVO 8000 Ethics Management Standard. Sections are further subdivided into subsections representing the organization's elements or activities.

ORGANIZATION CONTACT INFORMATION

XXX, Inc. is located at:

ETHICS POLICY AND OBJECTIVES

1.2 XXX, INC. ETHICS POLICY

1.1.1 Decision-making and accountability.

XXX, Inc. is an organization of decision makers. Decisions made at all levels in XXX will satisfy the following conditions:

- Decision makers will know that a decision must be made.
- Decision makers will know that decisions must be made within specific periods of time.
- Decision makers will confront a small number of well-defined options.
- Decision makers will know what is needed to make good decision.
- Decision makers will accept responsibility for their decisions.

XXX decision makers must consider their impact on an entire project. Moreover, other personnel involved in the decision (perhaps with only fragmentary knowledge of a particular organizational process), must be alert for irresponsible or unethical practices and take appropriate action when discovered.

1.1.2 Implementation

The Corporate Responsibility Management System Management Representative, who reports directly to the President/CEO, is hereby assigned the responsibility and authority to organize, maintain, and monitor the Corporate Responsibility Management System and to ensure its effective implementation.

All XXX, Inc. personnel are given the responsibility and authority to identify problems, and recommend solutions to those problems. It is the responsibility of each employee to bring to the attention of the cognizant vice president, any unethical practice immediately upon discovery.

Under the President/CEO, all vice presidents, directors, and the Management Representative comprise the Ethics Management Steering Committee and will function as defined herein.

Each division, under its Vice President, will implement the Corporate Responsibility Management System within its area of responsibility.

The President/CEO will resolve any conflicts which cannot be resolved by the vice presidents or the Corporate Responsibility Management System Management Representative. Resolution of such conflicts will always be in accordance with the requirements of the MVO 8000 International Standard and the XXX Corporate Responsibility Management System.

The Corporate Responsibility Management System objectives which follow are measurable and will be reviewed at all Management Review meetings, with revisions issued as appropriate.

1.2.3 Corporate Responsibility Management System Objectives

The following initial objectives inaugurate this Corporate Responsibility Management System (EMS). They will be reviewed at Management Review meetings and formally revised/ replaced in subsequent revisions to this Manual.

1. Implement/revise annual ethics training for all personnel. Document attendance. (NOV 2014).
2. Implement /revise the Code of Ethics and Standards of Conduct (June 2014).
3. Determine the level of training, experience, and competence of XXX personnel and develop a plan to provide additional required training (JUN 2014).
4. Reduce the length of time between origin of a reported ethics violation and its correction by 10% (NOV 2014).
5. Enhance employee recognition programs to further encourage contributions to corporate ethics and continual improvement of the Corporate Responsibility Management System (JUN 2014).

_____ Date: _____

President

1.4 GENERAL

XXX, Inc.'s Corporate Responsibility Management System reflects the ethical roles and responsibilities of all our operations, customer relations, and impacts on the community, as well as our commitment to all statutory and regulatory requirements. The requirements of the MVO 8000 Standard that are not applicable to our business are excluded from the scope of the Corporate Responsibility Management System.

Exclusion of an MVO 8000 requirement is permissible only when both of the following conditions are satisfied:

- The requirement must be limited to MVO 8000 Clause 7.
- Exclusion of the requirement will not affect our ability or responsibility to provide product that meets customer and applicable regulatory requirements.

Our authorized exclusions from the MVO 8000 Standard are as follows.

Exclusion:

Explanation:
There are no other exceptions.

1.5 INTERACTION WITH THE XXX, INC. QUALITY MANAGEMENT SYSTEM

The processes described in the Quality Management System Manual, along with all associated Operational Procedures (OPs) and flowcharts are subject to our Corporate Responsibility Management System.

The Management Representative maintains documents that identify all processes and, in conjunction with the appropriate Group and Program Managers, defines the relationships within these processes. Processes for management activities, provision of resources, product and service realization, and measurement are included, as well as methods needed to ensure the operation and control of processes is effective. These processes will be managed in accordance with the requirements of the International Standard(s) defined elsewhere.

Management will ensure the availability of resources to support the operation and monitoring of processes through regular interaction with department managers and through review of activities at

Management Review meetings. Vice Presidents, Group and Program Managers, Directors, and the Management Representative will monitor, measure, and analyze processes, and implement any actions necessary to achieve intended results and continual improvement. Results will also be discussed at Management Review meetings.

Outsourced processes may affect our product's conformance to requirements, and shall be controlled. The Management Representative and appropriate management personnel are responsible for defining the methods to control outsourced processes in procedures.

1.5.1 General Process Sequence Flow

Figure 1 describes operation of the Corporate Responsibility Management System.

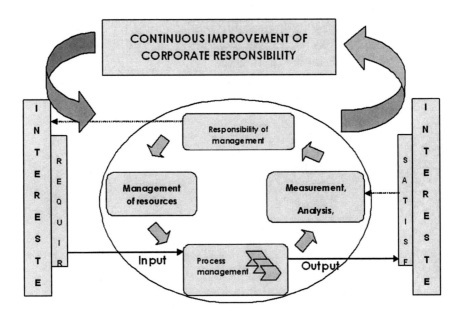

1.5.2 Documentation

Management will develop, document, implement, and continually improve a Corporate Responsibility Management System relevant to its business operations. Specifically, we will:

a) Monitor, measure, and analyze the System

b) Implement corrective and preventive action as necessary.

Corporate Responsibility Management System documentation will consist of an ethics manual containing documented explanations of ethics policies and objectives, and procedures required by this Standard.

1.5.3 The Corporate Responsibility Management Manual

The organization will establish and maintain a Corporate Responsibility System policy manual that includes:

a) The scope of the Corporate Responsibility System,

b) The documented procedures established for the system or reference to them, and

c) A description of the interaction between the processes of the Corporate Responsibility System.

SECTION 2: RESPONSIBILITIES

Figure 1 describes the organization of XXX, Inc. The responsibilities for the Corporate Responsibility Management System are described below.

XXX, Inc. Organization Chart

(INSERT

ORGANIZATION

CHART)

2.1 Involvement of Management

Management will demonstrate its ethical involvement with respect to customers, suppliers, company personnel, external board members (as applicable), other stakeholders, and the community by:

a) Communicating to all levels in the organization the importance of satisfying the requirements, standards, and values used by the organization to carry out its business,

b) Communicating to all levels in the organization the importance of satisfying statutory and regulatory requirements in the practice of company ethics,

c) Implementing the company's ethics policies and objectives,

d) Carrying out a program of internal reviews.

2.2 Corporate Responsibility Management Policy

Management will determine a policy and ensure that the policy formulated:

a) Is suitable and contiguous with the needs of the organization,

b) Is consistent with statutory and regulatory requirements,

c) Provides for continuous improvement of the Corporate Responsibility System.

2.2.1 Statutory and Regulatory Requirements

XXX, Inc. will identify statutory and regulatory requirements applicable to its operations.

2.3 Administration and Management

Management will establish:

a) The tasks, responsibilities, and authorities of all employees with respect to carrying out the formulated ethics policy

b) The tasks, responsibilities, and authorities of assigned supporting contractors, as applicable.

2.3.1 Oversight Officer/Management Representative

Management will appoint an individual responsible for the development, implementation, and maintenance of the Corporate Responsibility Management System; who reports directly to the Chief Executive and periodically reports on the performance of the Corporate Responsibility Management System and identifies potential improvements.

2.3.2 Internal Communication

Management will provide a structure to inform personnel about the Corporate Responsibility System, in which communication takes place at all levels and functions regarding the effectiveness of the Corporate Responsibility System.

2.4 Management Oversight

Management will periodically review the effectiveness of the Corporate Responsibility Management System and determine whether or not:

a) The System has to be modified,

b) Policies have to be modified, or objectives amended,

c) There is a need for corrective and preventive actions.

3. HUMAN RESOURCES

3.1.1 Human Resources

XXX, Inc. will train all personnel on the Corporate Responsibility Management System, its importance to our ethical operation, and how it applies to their positions and functions.

3.1.2 Ethics Awareness Training

Management will:

a) Develop and schedule Corporate Responsibility awareness training for all personnel,
b) Record and evaluate all training activities related to the Corporate Responsibility Management System.

3.1.3 Complaints Procedure

Management will provide employees with a process for communicating instances of unacceptable behavior, to include:

a) The complaint submission procedure
b) Responsibilities for complaints procedure administration,
c) Confidentiality of complaints,
d) Appeal rights of personnel accused.

3.1.4 Personnel Representation

Management will create a committee within the organization:

a) To monitor the ethical functioning of the organization,
b) To define objectives, tasks, responsibilities, authorities, and procedures in the operation of the Corporate Responsibility System, and
c) To review instances of reported violations, and
d) To administer the organization's sanctions (see 3.2).

3.2 Sanctions

In order to manage and prevent unacceptable ethical behavior, the organization will develop a system of sanctions to include:

a) Definition and description undesirable ethical behavior in the organization,
b) The manner in which unacceptable ethical conduct is reported,

c) The manner in which corrective action will be taken, and

d) The manner in which personal information is documented and recorded.

3.3 Code of Ethics and Standards of Conduct

Management will create a Code of Ethics and Standards of Conduct, to include (as applicable):

a) The Corporate Responsibility Management System

b) Statutory and regulatory requirements

c) Financial integrity and accurate disclosure

d) Formal standards of performance and expectations

e) Harassment

f) Staffing policies

g) The organization's approach to personnel customers, competitors, suppliers, and community

h) Unacceptable ethical behavior as it applies to the organization

i) Legal obligations of the organization and its members

j) Intellectual property

k) Physical and environmental security

l) Access control

m) Proper recording or and disbursement of funds or other assets

n) Use of company and customer property

o) Internet usage

p) Drug and substance abuse policy

q) Public communication

r) Working from home,

s) Internal auditing processes

t) Political contributions

u) Preparation of resumes

v) Wage determinations and gifts and gratuities.

SECTION 4: THE CORPORATE RESPONSIBILITY MANAGEMENT SYSTEM PROCESS

Figure 2 describes the Corporate Responsibility Management System Process.

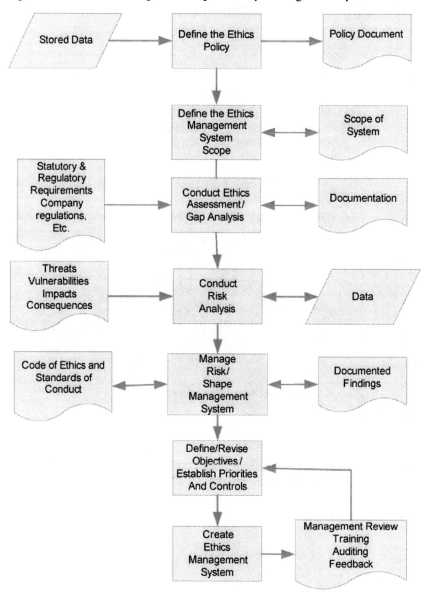

4 CORPORATE RESPONSIBILITY MANAGEMENT SYSTEM REQUIREMENTS

When any organization becomes disconnected from its customers and employees, as it can when focused on pursuit of profit, it can become complacent in its moral and ethical responsibilities. Employees, sensing a loss of importance and respect, will disconnect themselves from what they are paid to do. A customer, seeing these disconnects (often in the form of poor performance), will lose trust in the company and look elsewhere. Trust is essential, and employees and customers can tell the difference between a company that has a genuine regard for their welfare and one that only pretends concern.

It is for this reason that XXX, Inc. has established and implemented the Corporate Responsibility Management System. We will continually strive to improve its effectiveness, in accordance with the requirements of the MVO 8000 Standard. Processes needed for the Corporate Responsibility Management System are identified and the sequence and interaction of these processes are determined. Criteria and methods needed to ensure the operation and control of these processes are determined together with ensuring availability of resources and information to support and monitor the processes. Procedures are in place to monitor, measure, and analyze these processes, and to implement actions to achieve planned results and continual improvement of these processes. Any processes that are outsourced are identified, and controlled within the Corporate Responsibility Management System.

4.1 General

Management will develop, document, implement, and improve a Corporate Responsibility Management System that will:

a) Identify all processes and interactions reflected in the Corporate Responsibility Management System,

b) Determine the interaction between these various processes,

c) Determine the (ethics-based) effectiveness criteria for the implementation and monitoring of these processes,

d) Show the availability of resources and information relevant to the processes,

e) Monitor, measure, and analyze the processes,

f) Take the necessary actions:

1) To achieve the planned objectives,

2) To implement corrective and preventive action, and

3) To continuously improve the processes.

1.2 Documentation Requirements

4.2.1 General

Corporate Responsibility Management System documentation will consist of a manual containing documented explanations of ethics policies and objectives, and procedures required by this Standard.

4.2.2 Control of documents.

A documented procedure will be specified detailing the way in which

a) Documents will be approved for suitability prior to being issued,

b) Documents are reviewed, updated as necessary, and re-approved,

c) Changes and revision status are identified,

d) Relevant versions of documents are made available for reference,

e) Documents are maintained legible and readily identifiable, and

f) The manner in which the inadvertent use of expired documents is prevented.

4.2.3 Corporate Responsibility Management System Manual

The organization will establish and maintain a Corporate Responsibility Management System manual that includes:

a) The scope of the Corporate Responsibility Management System,

b) The documented procedures established for the system or reference to them, and

c) A description of the interaction between the processes of the Corporate Responsibility Management System.

To fulfil the requirements of the Corporate Responsibility Management System, XXX, Inc. will:

a) Identify the processes needed for the Corporate Responsibility Management System and their application throughout the organization,

b) Determine the sequence and interaction of these processes,

c) Determine criteria and methods needed to ensure that both the operation and control of these processes are effective,

d) Ensure the availability of resources and information necessary to support the operation and monitoring of these processes,

e) Monitor, measure, and analyze these processes, and

f) Implement actions necessary to achieve planned results and continual improvement of these processes.

XXX personnel have access to the manual via the Company Employee Website (READ ONLY) and will be notified of changes via e-mail. Copies may be printed for discussion and audit purposes (internal & external), but these are deemed to be uncontrolled documents. Distribution of the controlled master copies are defined in the "MANUAL CONTROL" section of this document.

Amendments

Any request for amendment of the Ethics Manual is referred to the Management Representative for review/approval. Prior to the issue of a revision, the Management Representative will review the amendment and authorize it for issue. A record of amendments is made on the Amendment Record. As new Amendment Record pages are needed, a suffix A, B, C etc. is added to the page number.

Reviews

The Manual is reviewed in accordance with the Corporate Responsibility Management System. It is also the basis for continual improvement at XXX, Inc. and is subject to ongoing review and revision.

1.1.4 Control of Records

Records are established and maintained to provide evidence of conformance to requirements and the effective operation of the

Corporate Responsibility Management System. Ethics Records shall be and remain legible, readily identifiable, and retrievable.

XXX has established a documented procedure for the identification, storage, protection, retrieval, retention time and disposition of Ethics records.

5. MANAGEMENT INVOLVEMENT

Successful companies respect customer and employee rights and expectations and find corporate profits and efficient management to be fully compatible with a fair and ethically responsible workplace environment. Management will perform its ethical responsibilities not only in a diligent manner, but in one that is standardized and consistent, as defined in this section.

5.1 Involvement of Management

Management will demonstrate its ethical involvement with customers, suppliers, company personnel, external board members (as applicable), other stakeholders, and the community by:

a) Developing, implementing, and continuously improving the Corporate Responsibility Management System,

b) Communicating to all levels in the organization the importance of satisfying the requirements, standards, and values used by the organization to carry out its business,

c) Communicating to all levels in the organization the importance of satisfying statutory and regulatory requirements in the practice of company ethics,

d) Developing and implementing the company's ethics policies and objectives,

e) Carrying out a program of internal audits, and

f) Making resources available.

5.2 Focus

Management will ensure that the needs and expectations of the organization with respect to social and ethical aspects in the organization are established.

5.3 Ethics Management Policy

Management will determine a policy and ensure that the policy formulated:

a) Is suitable and contiguous with the needs of the organization,

b) Is consistent with statutory and regulatory requirements,

c) Provides for continuous improvement of the Corporate Responsibility Management System

d) Provides the framework for measurable objectives,

e) Is communicated to, and understood by the whole organization, and

f) Is periodically assessed for its suitability.

5.4 Planning

Planning will be sufficient to address the requirements the Corporate Responsibility Management System.

5.4.1 Objectives

Management will formulate measurable objectives for all relevant functions and levels of the organization, to ensure the efficiency and continual improvement of the Corporate Responsibility Management System. Objectives will be consistent with Corporate Responsibility Management System policies and responsibilities and appropriate personnel will be assigned completion dates for action items.

5.4.2 Statutory and Regulatory Requirements

Management will identify statutory and regulatory requirements applicable to its operations.

5.5 Administration and Management

Management will ensure that all responsibilities and authorities are documented and communicated through the organization. Management will establish:

a) The tasks, responsibilities, and authorities of all employees with respect to carrying out the formulated ethics policy.

b) The tasks, responsibilities, and authorities of assigned supporting contractors, as applicable.

5.5.1 Management Representative

Management will appoint a management representative, who will be responsible for the development, implementation, and maintenance of the Corporate Responsibility Management System.

The Management Representative will report directly to the Chief Executive and periodically report on the performance of the

Corporate Responsibility Management System and identify potential improvements.

1.1.2 Internal Communication

Management will provide a structure to inform personnel about the Corporate Responsibility Management System, in which communication takes place at all levels and functions regarding the effectiveness of the Corporate Responsibility Management System.

5.6 Management Review

Management will periodically review the effectiveness of the Corporate Responsibility Management System. During each review, management will determine:

a) If the Corporate Responsibility Management System has to be modified,
b) If policies have to be modified, or objectives amended,
c) The need for (or status of) corrective and corrective actions.

5.6.1 Management Review Input

The input for the Management Review will include:

a) Corporate Responsibility Management System audit/review findings,
b) External and internal feedback,
c) Corrective and preventive measures that have been taken,
d) The status of actions and decisions from previous meetings,
e) Planned changes to the Corporate Responsibility Management System,
f) Customer feedback, and
g) Recommendations for improvements.

5.6.2 Management Review Output

The output from the Management Review will include:

a) Decisions and action points for improvement,
b) Decisions and actions in response to inputs, and
c) Decisions and action points with respect to the resources needed.

6. RESOURCE MANAGEMENT

Fairness in all matters dealing with customers and company personnel requires, at least, that policies, standards, and decisions be directly related to customers and company personnel, based on clear and available data, and applied equally.

6.1 Provision of Resources

In developing the Corporate Responsibility Management System, management will:

a) Determine and allocate all resources required,
b) Ensure that required resources are made available,
c) Ensure that all personnel are aware of the resources available to them.

6.2 Human Resources

6.2.1 General

Personnel will be trained on the Corporate Responsibility Management System and how it applies to their positions and functions, and the impact ethically inappropriate performance has on XXX, Inc.

6.2.2 Awareness Training

Management will:

a) Develop and schedule ethics awareness training for all personnel,
b) Evaluate and measure the effectiveness of the training, and
c) Record all relevant training conducted.

6.2.3 Complaints Procedure

Management will provide employees with a process for communicating instances of unacceptable behavior, to include:

a) The complaint submission procedure
b) Responsibilities for complaint procedure administration,
c) Confidentiality of complaints,
d) Appeal rights of personnel accused.

6.2.3 Personnel Representation

Management will create a committee within the organization:

a) To monitor the ethical functioning of the organization,
b) To define objectives, tasks, responsibilities, authorities, and procedures in the operation of the Corporate Responsibility Management System,
c) To review instances of reported violations, and
d) To administer the organization's sanctions.

6.3 Sanctions

In order to manage and prevent unacceptable ethical behavior, the organization will develop a system of sanctions to include:

a) Definition and description undesirable ethical behavior in the organization,
b) The manner in which unacceptable ethical conduct is reported,
c) The manner in which corrective action will be taken, and
d) The manner in which personal information is documented nd recorded.

6.4 Code of Ethics and Standards of Conduct.

Management will implement a Code of Ethics and Standards of Conduct, to include (as applicable):

a) The Corporate Responsibility Management System
b) Statutory and regulatory requirements
c) Financial integrity and accurate disclosure
d) Formal standards of performance and expectations
e) Harassment
f) Staffing policies
g) The organization's approach to personnel customers, competitors, suppliers, and community
h) Unacceptable ethical behavior as it applies to the organization
i) Legal obligations of the organization and its members
j) Intellectual property
k) Physical and environmental security
l) Access control
m) Proper recording or and disbursement of funds or other assets

n) Use of company and customer property
o) Internet usage
p) Drug and substance abuse policy
q) Public communication
r) Working from home,
s) Internal auditing processes
t) Political contributions
u) Preparation of resumes
v) Wage determinations and gifts and gratuities.

7. PROCESS MANAGEMENT

How management conducts itself in the workplace can do more to enhance or diminish the work environment and, in turn, the quality of the ultimate product or service. XXX, Inc. management at all levels will ensure that all processes and interactions required in product or service realization conform or exceed our stated ethical values, standards, and objectives.

1.1 Communication and Participation

Management will involve all levels of the organization in the operation of the Corporate Responsibility Management System.

a) Committees will ensure that meetings are recorded, and
b) Sufficient time and resources are allocated.

1.2 Integrity and Disclosure

Management will define (as applicable) processes for:

a) Financial integrity and accurate disclosure
b) Key performance indicators and reporting of deviations
c) Management responsibilities and review
d) Safeguards (e.g., periodic inventories, reconciliations,)
e) Record keeping and retention
f) Recording and disbursement of funds
g) Risk analysis and mitigation
h) Conflicts of interests, outside interests, and related transactions
i) Timesheet and travel claim preparation, to include:
   1) Time recording
   2) Labor charging/rate determination
   3) Customer billing
j) Copyrighted or licensed materials
k) Accurate representation of data and credentials
l) Reporting adverse personnel information.

1.3 Personnel Recruitment and Selection

The organization will develop ethically responsible procedures for the recruitment and selection of personnel so as to positively influence and reinforce company culture. The organization will implement and maintain the following as applicable:

a) A policy statement precluding discrimination on grounds of ethnic origin, handicap or gender or other discrimination,

b) A signed agreement by prospective employees adhering to the Statement of Ethics Policy,

c) A documented selection procedure for employment agencies servicing the organization,

d) Criteria for evaluation of the ethics of employment agencies doing business with the organization,

e) Recording the results of the measures.

7.4 Contracts of Employment (If Applicable)

All contracts and contracting actions will reflect our Code of Ethics and Standards of Conduct.

7.5 Performance Review

Management will ensure that scheduled personnel performance reviews cover adherence to the policies and practices of the Corporate Responsibility Management System. Specifically:

a) The organization will describe the procedures for carrying out the above-mentioned appraisal / performance discussion, in its regulations.

b) Discussion will cover all areas and issues that can affect the work and the performance of the employee.

c) The employee to be appraised must be informed about what is required of him or her in the function that he or she is carrying out.

d) The organization will produce a standard appraisal form for use by reporting seniors in the organization, and

e) An appeals procedure.

1.6 Requirements for Suppliers/Subcontractors

XXX. Inc. will ensure that its suppliers and subcontractors are aware of the applicable sections of our Corporate Responsibility Management System, specifically:

a) What we expect of our suppliers and subcontractors, and

b) What they have the right to expect from us.

7.7 Community Responsibility

XXX. Inc. will develop a policy defining its responsibility to the community (i.e., district, town/city, and state/region).

7.8 Quality of Life

XXX. Inc. will monitor its effect on the quality of life of:
- a) Employees and their families,
- b) The geographical area or community in which we operate and our potential to impact positively or negatively in that area or community.

7.9 Competition

XXX. Inc. will conform to applicable statutory and regulatory requirements with regard to:
- a) The development and maintenance of pricing structures,
- b) Delivery terms and conditions,
- c) Exclusion of supply to particular customers,
- d) The use of different prices for the same level of performance.
- e) Doing business with organizations that use restrictive competitive practices,
- f) The fixing of prices,
- g) Dividing of markets, and
- h) Restrictive production or supply practices.

7.10 Accident Reporting

Management will develop procedures for the prompt and comprehensive reporting of safety or environmental accidents to proper authorities.

7.11 Hazardous Materials

XXX. Inc. will develop (as applicable) procedures to prevent or reduce the environmental risks related to the storage, transfer, and transport of dangerous materials, to include:
- a) National laws and regulations, guidelines, decisions, and permits,
- b) Responsibilities for carrying out formulated policy,

c) Procedures for the storage, transfer and transport of dangerous materials,
d) Training and qualifications of users.

7.12 Pollution Prevention

XXX. Inc. will develop pollution prevention procedures to include (as applicable):

a) Identification of all potential sources of pollution, wastes, and emissions,
b) Identification of all applicable statutory and regulatory requirements.
c) Reduction or mitigation measures
d) Recycling opportunities.

XXX. Inc. will discuss the operation of the pollution prevention procedures at scheduled Management Reviews and record discussions, nonconformities, and corrective and preventive actions.

7.13 Energy Conservation

XXX. Inc. will develop an Energy Conservation Program, to include (as applicable):

a) An energy conservation policy,
b) A survey identifying all sources of energy expenditure and the technical and economic feasibility of implementing specific energy conservation measures.
c) Periodic evaluation of the system during the internal audits and management reviews.

7.14 Environmental Assessment

XXX, Inc. will carry out, or have carried out a survey of the environmental aspects of the activities, and alternatives for those activities which may constitute potential harm to the environment.

7.14.1 Environmental Aspects

XXX, Inc. will identify all relevant environmental aspects of products and services, to include (as applicable):

a) A purchasing policy reflecting for products and services with potential environmental impact

b) Criteria and selection of the most suitable products and suppliers

c) Possible substitutions for products having the potential to harm the environment.

7.15 Competence, Experience, and Training

XXX, Inc. will establish requirements with regard to the education and instruction of all personnel and, in addition, will set standards for competence, experience, and training in the following areas related to the Corporate Responsibility Management System:

a) Occupational Safety and Health,
b) Energy conservation
c) Hazardous Material Control and Management
d) Pollution prevention
e) Recycling
f) Contracting
g) Procurement
h) Internal auditing
i) Finance and accounting.

7.16 Risk Assessment and Minimization

XXX, Inc. will implement risk assessment and minimization procedures for all activities and components in order to:

a) Determine and track Risk as a function of threats, criticalities, and vulnerabilities to its missions
b) Determine a relative ranking of potential risks, and determine the likely frequencies and consequences of those risks,
c) Recognize opportunities as well as risks, and
d) Formalize and document knowledge for more precise decision-making.

7.17 Emergency Preparedness and Response

XXX, Inc. will develop an emergency response plan covering (as applicable):

a) Identification of potential disasters or emergencies in the organization
b) Preplanned responses
c) Emergency evacuation, aid, and assistance,
d) Safeguarding organization personnel

e) Consequence management (including drills or exercises)
f) Disaster prevention,
g) Cooperation with external aid and assistance organizations
h) Employee awareness training
i) Emergency reporting.

7.18 Absence Due to Illness

XXX, Inc. will develop and implement procedures to investigated and reduce work related absenteeism and incapacity through illness, to include:

a) The definition of work related absenteeism and incapacity through illness.
b) Information and training for managers regarding absenteeism, and ways to address employee illness, absence, and return,
c) Maintenance of absenteeism statistics, and
d) Work related health investigation.

7.19 Safety and Health

XXX, Inc. will develop and implement a safety and health promotion policy, to include (as applicable):

a) Occupational safety,
b) Accident prevention and safe human behavior,
c) Workplace cleanliness and sanitation (including ventilation systems),
d) Exercise and nutrition,
e) Transportation safety.

7.20 Working hours

XXX. Inc. will develop and implement policies regarding working hours, to include:

a) Applicable statutory and regulatory requirements,
b) Core working hours,
c) Employee categories,
d) Emergency recalls,
e) Working from home,
f) Overtime, and
g) Project time and billing (if appropriate).

8. MEASUREMENT, ANALYSIS, AND IMPROVEMENT

We will measure corporate performance at XXX, Inc. in order to ensure adherence to our standards of ethics, corporate performance, and the rules and regulations of higher authority.

8.1 General

XXX. Inc. will establish and maintain documented procedures to monitor and measure, on a regular basis, the key characteristics of its operations and activities that can have significant impact on the professional and business ethics of the organization.

8.0.1 Personnel, Customer, and Stakeholder Satisfaction

XXX, Inc. will develop a research methodology for periodic measurement of personnel, board, and stakeholders' satisfaction, to include:

a) Effectiveness of the Corporate Responsibility Management System,
b) Effectiveness of the Code of Ethics and Standards of Conduct,
c) Personnel, customer, and stakeholder feedback.

8.1.2 Internal Reviews/Audits

XXX, Inc. will conduct periodic internal reviews to determine the effectiveness of the Corporate Responsibility Management System. Reviews will be scheduled based on the nature and importance of the activities and the results from previous audits.

Internal auditing will be conducted in order to:

a) Determine whether or not the Corporate Responsibility Management System:
   1) Conforms to the organization's requirements and to statutory and regulatory requirements
   2) Has been properly implemented and maintained
b) Provide information on the results of audits to management.

Audit procedures shall cover audit scope, frequency, and methodologies, as well as the responsibilities and requirements for conducting audits and reporting results.

8.1 Nonconformance and Corrective and Preventive Action

XXX, Inc. will establish and maintain procedures for defining responsibility and authority for ethical nonconformities, taking action to mitigate any impacts caused and for initiating and completing corrective and preventive action.

Corrective or preventive action taken to eliminate the cause of actual of potential nonconformities will be appropriate for the magnitude of the problem and commensurate with actual or potential impact.

8.3 Continual Improvement

XXX. Inc. will continually assess and improve the effectiveness of the Corporate Responsibility Management System through the use of:
  a) Policies and objectives
  b) Audit results
  c) Data analyses and market research
  d) Personnel, customer, and stakeholders' satisfaction
  e) Corrective and preventive measures
  f) Management review meetings.

When shortcomings are detected from audit results, data analyses, satisfaction surveys, or management reviews, the organization will ensure that timely corrective and preventive measures are taken.

XXX, Inc. will document the effectiveness of measures taken.

8.4 Records

XXX. Inc. will establish and maintain procedures for the identification, maintenance, and disposition of records that relate to the Corporate Responsibility Management System. These records shall include training records and the results of audits and reviews.

Records will be legible, identifiable, and traceable to the activity involved. Records will be stored in order to be readily retrievable and protected against damage. Records will also be stored in such a way as to maintain confidentiality.

Physical storage of the records will be such as to demonstrate conformance with this Standard.

RECOMMENDED READINGS AND REFERENCES

1.   International Standard, MVO 8000, Ethics *Management Systems—Requirements*, Boca Raton, FL: International Certification Registrars, 2006

2.   ANSI/ISO/ASQ Q9001-2008 American National Standard, *Quality Management Systems and Requirements*, Milwaukee, WI: ASQ Quality Press, 2008

3.   ANSI/ISO/ASQ Q9004-*2008* American National Standard *Quality Management Systems—Guidelines for Performance Improvements*, Milwaukee, WI, ASQ Quality Press, 2008

4.   ANSI/ISO/ASQ E14001-*2004 Environmental Management Systems—Requirements with Guidance foe Use*, Milwaukee, WI, ASQ Quality Press, 2004

5.   Andersen, Bjorn, *Bringing Business Ethics to Life, Achieving Corporate Social Responsibility*, Milwaukee, WI: American Society for Quality, 2004

6.   Coles, Robert, Lives of Moral Leadership, New York, Random House, 2008

7.   Deal, Terrence E. And Kennedy, Allan A, Corporate Cultures, *The Rites and Rituals of Corporate Life*, Cambridge, MA: Perseus Books Publishing, 2008

8.   Cloud, Dr. Henry, *Integrity, The Courage to Meet the Demands of Reality*, New York: Harper Collins, 2006

9.   Frankena, Wm. K, *Ethics*, Englewood Cliffs, NJ: Prentice-Hall, Inc., 1963

10.   Lander, Guy P, *What is Sarbanes-Oxley?*, New York: McGraw-Hill, 2004

11.   Green, Scott, *Manager's Guide to the Sarbanes-Oxley Act, Improving Internal Controls to Prevent Fraud*. Hoboken, NJ: John Wiley & Sons, 2004

12.   *Harvard Business Review on Corporate Strategy*, Boston, MA: Harvard Business School Press, 1999

13.   Piskurich, George M, ET. al (Ed), *The ASTD Handbook Design and Delivery*, New York: McGraw-Hill, 2004

14.   Laird, Dugan, *Approaches to Training and Development, 2nd Ed*, Cambridge, MA: Perseus Publishing, 1985

15.   Drucker, Peter F, *Managing in the Next Society*, New York: Truman Talley Books, 2002

16.   Stonich, Paul J, (Ed) Implementing Strategy, Making Strategy

Happen, Cambridge MA, Ballenger Publishing Co. 1982

17.   Shore, Bill, The Light of Conscience, How a Simple Act Can Change Your Life, New York: Random House, 2004

18.   Haliibozek, Edward, Jones, Andy, and Kovacioch, Gerald L, *The Corporate Security Professional's Handbook on Terrorism,* Burlington, MA: Butterworth-Heinemann, Inc, 2008

19.   Canton, Lucien G, *Emergency Management, Concepts and Strategies for Effective Programs,* Hoboken, NJ: John Wiley & Sons, 2007

About the Author:

Eugene A. (Gene) Razzetti retired from the U.S. Navy as a Captain in 1992, a decorated Vietnam Veteran and having had two at-sea and two major shore commands. Since then, he has been an independent management consultant, project manager, and auditor. He became a military analyst after September 11, 2001. He co-authored MVO 8000, the Corporate Responsibility Management Standard that is contained in this publication. He is also the author of <u>Fixes That Last—The Executive's Guide to Fix It or Lose It Management</u>. He is a frequent contributor to management journals on subjects such as Strategic Planning, Risk Management, Information Security, Supply Chain Security, and Environmental Systems Management; and currently serves on the advisory boards of two schools of business.

He has served on many boards and committees dealing with ethics and professionalism in the practice of management consulting.

CPSIA information can be obtained at www.ICGtesting.com
Printed in the USA
BVOW08s0423200913

331645BV00001B/4/P